THE NEW ENGLAND SEAFOOD MARKETS COOKBOOK

THE NEW ENGLAND SEAFOOD MARKETS COOKBOOK

RECIPES FROM THE BEST LOBSTER POUNDS, CLAM SHACKS, AND FISHMONGERS

MIKE URBAN

THE COUNTRYMAN PRESS
A DIVISION OF W. W. NORTON & COMPANY
Independent Publishers Since 1923

For information about permission to reproduce selections from this book, write to Permissions, The Countryman Press, 500 Fifth Avenue, New York, NY 10110

For information about special discounts for bulk purchases, please contact W. W. Norton Special Sales at specialsales@wwnorton.com or 800-233-4830

Manufacturing by Versa Press
Book design by Endpaper Studio

The Countryman Press
www.countrymanpress.com

A division of W. W. Norton & Company, Inc.
500 Fifth Avenue, New York, N.Y. 10110
www.wwnorton.com

978-1-58157-324-4 (pbk.)

10 9 8 7 6 5 4 3 2 1

To Sylvia, Elaine, and Carl

Richie Taylor, Wulf's Fish Market, Brookline, Massachusetts

Acknowledgments

First and foremost, I'd like to give my heartfelt thanks to the numerous seafood market owners and workers who took time out of their busy days (especially during summer) to take me into their shops, show me their operations, and most important, share their favorite recipes and stories for inclusion in this book. I've made many new friends along the way, and I've learned a lot, for which I'm very grateful.

I'd also like to thank the crew at Countryman Press—Senior Editor Dan Crissman, Editorial Director Ann Treistman, and Publicist Devorah Backman—for their patience and support as I cruised up and down the New England seaboard, gathering information and recipes and photographing the seafood and the markets during the research and writing of this book. I cherish my relationship with Countryman, which published two of my previous books on the lobster shacks and the diners of New England.

Finally, I thank my wife, Ellen, who kept things running smoothly at home while I was away (in addition to her full-time job as managing editor of the Globe Pequot Press) and whose support and encouragement keep me going on these seemingly endless book projects from one year to the next. Je t'aime!

—*Mike Urban*

Contents

Introduction

New England has a long, colorful history of harvesting the bounty of the nearby sea. The fish and shellfish from New England's bays, estuaries, sounds, and gulfs play a major role in what is considered to be one of the region's authentic cuisines. New England seafood is prized locally, throughout the region, around the country, and throughout the world—think chowder, lobster rolls, codfish cakes, shad, haddock, and fried clams. From the once endless bounty of the almighty cod to the wildly popular and currently plentiful stocks of Maine lobster, there's much to celebrate in the way of New England seafood.

This book contains some 150 recipes from more than forty of New England's finest independently owned and operated seafood markets. Most of the markets are simple family operations, and many have been in business for decades. The retailers rely on their customers, who are passionate about locally harvested seafood and who in turn count on their local fishmongers to deliver the freshest fish available. Customers also turn to fish market owners for guidance on how to prepare all sorts of tasty, innovative dishes that are steeped in tradition, as well as for recipes that represent more contemporary tastes and trends in seafood cookery.

The recipes contained herein include many that New England's seafood market owners recommend to their customers—as well as some that come from the owners' home kitchens. There's a lot of love in these recipes, and it shines through in many different ways—from the unique ingredients needed to prepare them to the fun, sometimes ingenious methods of cooking called upon to create authentic New England seafood cuisine.

The book is organized by types of dishes (soups and chowders, starters, salads, pasta dishes, grilled seafood, stews and casseroles, and more) and by types of seafood (lobster, swordfish, salmon, tuna, cod, haddock, shrimp, and clams), so there is plenty to explore on this culinary journey through the region. There's a special chapter at the end entitled "New England Exotica," which contains unusual dishes, mostly indigenous and unique to the region, as well as some other recipes that are further afield in terms of their seafood ingredients and cultural heritages.

Have fun perusing these pages and trying out these recipes, which come from people who truly live, breathe, and love New England seafood every day of their lives. There's plenty to learn and to enjoy on this journey through one of the richest seafood cultures in the world.

SOUPS AND CHOWDERS

Cappy's Clear-Broth Clam Chowder

Flanders Fish Market, East Lyme, Connecticut

2 large Spanish onions, peeled and diced

¼ cup olive oil

12 quahog clams, shucked, with clam meat and juice set aside

2 cups chopped ocean clams (fresh is best, but canned will do)

3 russet potatoes, peeled and cut to medium dice

2 quarts clam juice (low sodium is best)

4 tablespoons cold butter, cut into large chunks

Coarse salt and fresh-ground black pepper

Fresh or dried parsley

Oyster crackers

Clam chowder in Connecticut and Rhode Island is often the clear-broth variety—unencumbered by thick, rich cream and lightly seasoned in a variety of ways. The clear-broth versions allow the pure clam flavor to take center stage in what many consider a more representative version of the New England staple. This simple version from an excellent seafood market in southeastern Connecticut substitutes olive oil for the usual salt pork, making for a healthier, more clam-infused broth.

In a heavy-bottomed stockpot, sauté the onions in the olive oil over medium heat until they're translucent, about 3 minutes. While the onions cook, chop the quahog clams to a rough mince. Add the quahogs and ocean clams to the onions and cook for 3 to 5 minutes, stirring continuously to combine. Add the potatoes to the clams, stir to combine, and allow the mixture to cook for 3 to 5 minutes.

Add all the clam juice and stir well to blend the ingredients evenly. Increase the heat to medium high and bring the chowder just to a boil. Cover the pot, reduce the heat to medium low, and allow the chowder to simmer for 45 to 60 minutes. Stir occasionally, until the potatoes are tender enough to fall apart and thicken the chowder a bit.

Just before serving, stir in the cold chunks of butter, and season to taste with salt and pepper. Garnish each dish with parsley and serve with oyster crackers. Serves 6 to 8.

Portuguese Fish Chowder

Anthony's Seafood, Middletown, Rhode Island

---

1 tablespoon lightly salted butter

2 tablespoons celery, diced

3 tablespoons onion, diced

1¼ cup chouriço, diced (smoked Portuguese sausage)

½ cup white wine

Pinch of red chili pepper flakes

Pinch of black pepper

½ tablespoon paprika

1 tablespoon Tabasco sauce

⅓ cup flour

2 cups clam juice

½ pound medium raw shrimp (shelled)

½ pound sea scallops, sliced

1 pound chunked codfish (or other white fish)

2½ cups potatoes, diced and cooked firm

3 teaspoons fresh parsley, chopped

3 to 4 cups half-and-half

Anthony's Portuguese Fish Chowder from Middletown, Rhode Island, is an amazing combination of flavors that always leaves you wanting more. Creamy, spicy, flavorful, and full of good seafood and spicy sausage, it's a meal unto itself and a crowd-pleasing comfort food.

Heat a heavy skillet to medium high and melt the butter. Sauté the celery, onions, and chouriço (pronounced shore-EEZ) until the vegetables are translucent and the chouriço is lightly cooked.

Add the white wine, chili flakes, pepper, paprika, and Tabasco, and mix together. Slowly add the flour, stirring constantly over medium-high heat to make a roux, until the mixture is dark and paste-like in consistency.

Add the clam juice and whisk vigorously until smooth. Add the shrimp, scallops, and codfish. Bring it to a simmer, then add the cooked potatoes and parsley. Before serving, slowly add the half-and-half, and heat until steaming, not boiling, stirring constantly. Serves 10 to 12.

Crab Chowder

Bayley's Lobster Pound, Scarborough, Maine

1 yellow onion, diced

2 stalks celery, diced

4 ounces (1 stick) butter

¾ cup flour

10 slices bacon, soft-cooked and chopped

5 medium potatoes, peeled, diced, and par-boiled for about 5 minutes

¼ cup fresh parsley, chopped

¼ teaspoon paprika

⅛ teaspoon garlic salt

⅛ teaspoon celery salt

⅛ teaspoon white pepper

1 teaspoon seafood seasoning

Salt and freshly ground black pepper

1 quart milk

1 pint heavy cream

1 can corn, drained

1 pound fresh crabmeat

Crabmeat is picked fresh all along the coast of Maine, much of it in the fall, when the crabs are larger and meatier. Maine crab is the preferred kind for this crab chowder recipe from Bayley's Lobster Pound in Scarborough, Maine. Peeky-toe crabmeat from rock crabs in the Penobscot Bay area is particularly prized among Mainers, so see if you can procure some of it for this nice variation on a standard New England–style chowder recipe.

In a medium soup pot, sauté the onion and celery in the melted butter over medium heat until translucent, about 2 minutes. Turn the heat to low, add the flour, and mix well until the mixture is pasty. Using a whisk, add the bacon, potatoes, parsley, paprika, garlic salt, celery salt, white pepper, seafood seasoning, and salt and pepper to taste. Mix, and then slowly add the milk and cream, stirring constantly. Add the corn, then gently fold in the crabmeat. Stir slowly. Serves 4 to 6.

Browne's Local Fish Chowder

Browne's Trading Market, Portland, Maine

2 large Spanish onions, finely diced

6 large celery stalks, finely diced

1 tablespoon dried thyme

3 tablespoons unsalted butter

3 cups fish stock

3 large Yukon Gold potatoes, cut into ½-inch cubes

2 quarts half-and-half

3 pounds locally caught (if possible) cod, haddock, hake, or halibut

Salt and freshly ground black pepper

Browne's refers to this chowder as "local" because it calls for locally caught fish. Any time you can use locally caught seafood in your cooking, you're most likely going to be healthier—and happier! (This chowder is in the classic Maine "milky" style—not too thick, not too thin, with lots of fresh-fish flavor.)

In a large, heavy-bottomed pot, sauté the onions, celery, and thyme in the butter over medium heat until they're softened. Add the fish stock and bring the mixture to a soft boil. Add the diced potatoes and cook until they're softened, about 10 minutes.

Turn the heat to medium-low and add the half-and-half. Heat and stir until steaming, then add the fish of your choice in whole fillets. Allow the fillets just a few minutes to cook and break apart.

Salt and pepper to taste, and serve immediately. Serves 10 as a main course.

Boothbay Lobster Wharf

Boothbay Harbor, Maine

This large lobster shack and fishing operation sits on pilings and heavy planks above the eastern shore of Boothbay Harbor. It's a very busy place, with its lobster boilers, seafood shack, numerous open-air picnic tables, full-service bar, and gift shop. Tourists mob the place in the summertime, and with good reason: Boothbay Lobster Wharf has one of the biggest and best lobster rolls in Mid-Coast Maine. A small fleet of lobster boats services the wharf, and the catch starts coming in around mid-day, guaranteeing that your lobster is going to be off-the-boat fresh.

Tucked away between a couple of the buildings is a small fish market with a limited but very nice selection of fresh-filleted fish and several types of shellfish. On any given day you'll find swordfish, salmon, haddock, scallops, clams, shrimp—and, of course, lobsters. The market will cook your lobsters for take-away, if you wish, and they keep a constant supply of fresh-picked lobster meat in the refrigerated case, in the event you want to forego the whole shell-cracking process.

Small though it may be, Boothbay Lobster Wharf Fish Market is a good thing to know about when you're vacationing in crowded, touristy Boothbay Harbor. You can get some really fresh fish at great prices, without fighting the crowds at larger markets in the area.

Lobster Chowder

Boothbay Lobster Wharf, Boothbay Harbor, Maine

2 pounds lobster meat, fresh-picked from approximately 8 pounds whole, cooked lobster (reserve as much liquid as possible from the picking)

2 pounds all-purpose or red potatoes, peeled or unpeeled, and cut into ½-inch cubes

½ cup (1 stick) butter

½ gallon whole milk

½ gallon half-and-half

½ teaspoon lobster base

Salt and pepper to taste

This wonderful lobster shack has a small retail fish market that deals mostly in fresh cod, haddock, and (of course) live lobsters, as well as a commanding view of Boothbay Harbor from its spacious decks. Owner Todd Simmons has a great recipe for a milky, Maine-style lobster chowder that's quite easy to make—except for picking all that fresh lobster meat, which is laborious. But fresh-picked lobster makes all the difference.

Boil or steam the lobsters until they're fully cooked. Set aside to cool for an hour or so, then pick all the lobster meat over a bowl, retaining as much of the water and juices as possible from the picking.

Fill a large stock-pot at least halfway with water, and heat it to boiling. Add the cubed potatoes and cook until they're tender, about 10 minutes. Drain the potatoes, then return them to the stock pot. Add the butter, then the whole milk and half-and-half, and slowly warm over medium heat, stirring occasionally.

When the contents of the pot begin to steam, add the lobster meat, the liquid from the picking, and the lobster base. Stir to combine and continue heating for 2 to 3 minutes, until the lobster meat is warmed through. Salt and pepper to taste, then remove the chowder from the heat and serve. Serves 8 to 10 dinner-size portions or 14 to 16 side bowls.

Clam Shack Seafood's Clam Chowder

Clam Shack Seafood Market, Kennebunk, Maine

2 cups sea clams, chopped (about 8 pounds in the shell, then cooked, shucked, and chopped)

1 teaspoon oil or butter

¼ pound salt pork, diced

1 large onion, diced

2 large potatoes, diced in ½-inch pieces

1 cup reserved clam broth (or clam juice)

3 cups heavy cream

Salt and pepper

Like most things at the Clam Shack's famous food stand, this chowder is a cut above, especially if you follow their suggestion to cook your clams from scratch.

This chowder is best when you cook the clams yourself. Try to cook them in saltwater whenever possible, to preserve the ocean flavor. If saltwater isn't nearby and available, give your rapidly boiling water a good shake of coarse salt. Toss in the clams, and tightly cover with a lid for three to five minutes or until all the shells are open. Discard any clams that don't open after cooking, and reserve the broth.

Melt the butter in a large pot, and sauté the salt pork in the butter until it's golden and fragrant. Add the onion and cook until it's translucent. Add the potatoes and cook for 3 minutes. Stir in the clam broth or juice and simmer for 25 minutes.

Add the cream and simmer until the potatoes are tender. Stir in the clams and simmer for 5 minutes. Season with salt and pepper. Serves 4.

Wulf's Fish Market

Brookline, Massachusetts

Wulf's is "old-school" in every good sense of the term. It presents its fish on ice-covered tabletops in its open-air store, making you feel you're at the same market in which your grandparents used to shop, unencumbered by plastic or glass partitions. This is a great place to get a good look at expertly filleted and whole fish fresh from New England waters and from around the world.

Wulf's Fish Market has a long and glorious history in the Brookline-Allston neighborhood of Boston, where it's been since 1926. Founder Sam Wulf purchased Berger's Fish Market on Harvard Street, renamed his new enterprise Wulf's, and proceeded to work there for the next forty-two years. Sam's son Alan joined the business upon his father's retirement, in 1968, and worked at Wulf's for the next forty-two years himself, until some health issues persuaded him to sell the store in 2010 (Alan still visits the market frequently).

There's still plenty of family in the business. Alan's nephew Richie Taylor has been a buyer/manager of Wulf's for the past forty years, and he shares these duties with Peter Ryan. One or both of them make daily trips in the early morning hours to the Boston Seaport, to inspect and purchase the freshest fish and shellfish they can find from incoming boats and airplane shipments. They bring their purchases back to the store and hand-cut all the fillets on large, wooden chopping-block tables, in full view of customers perusing the displays of fresh fish in the shop.

Alan, Richie, and Peter have stuck stubbornly to Wulf's time-honored tradition of purchasing only what looks best at the market in Boston each day. This sometimes makes it difficult to plan your fish-purchasing decisions at Wulf's, but you're guaranteed the freshest fish anywhere. While you're perusing the day's offerings on the tabletop displays, Richie and Pete and the rest of the staff are right there at the cutting tables, dressed in their old-fashioned starched-white shirts and

Richie Taylor

aprons, ready to answer any questions you may have or to suggest the best methods for preparing any fish or shellfish they may be selling that day.

The display tables sit right up by the pane-glass windows fronting the street, and curious passersby constantly stop to check out the day's offerings through the glass. The staples, such as cod, haddock, salmon, halibut, monkfish, flounder, redfish, and sole, can be found nearly every day. Available seasonally are items such as striped bass, branzini (European sea bass), bluefish, soft shell crabs, and certain freshwater fish brought in special for the Jewish high holidays (see the recipe for gefilte fish on the next page). There is also a wide variety of smoked fish: salmon, bluefish, whitefish, sable, haddock, and herring.

Wulf's is truly a blast from the past, and it clings to its time-honored traditions of hand-selecting only the finest fish available each day and presenting them as few other New England fish markets do. Treat yourself to some of their fine wares, even if you have to ice them down and truck them home yourself. You won't regret it!

Wulf's Gefilte Fish

Wulf's Fish Market, Brookline, Massachusetts

5 pounds whole freshwater fish (carp, pike, or whitefish work well)

2 onions, finely chopped

1 teaspoon sugar

2 eggs, well beaten

1½ teaspoons salt

1 teaspoon pepper

1½ teaspoons matzo meal

¼ cup cold water

BROTH

Heads and bones from whole fish

Salt and pepper to taste

6 large carrots, peeled and sliced

2 large onions, sliced

Gefilte fish translates from the Yiddish as "stuffed fish," a practice that is increasingly rare these days. Today, gefilte fish appears most commonly in the form of ground up whitefish, rolled into balls and boiled in a broth, and it's still a staple in many Jewish households during holidays and family gatherings. In this recipe, from Richie Taylor of Wulf's Fish Market, virtually no part of the fish goes to waste in the preparation of the fish balls and broth.

Debone and then grind the fish meat in a grinder or food processor. Set the bones aside for the broth.

In a large bowl, mix together the ground fish, onions, sugar, eggs, salt, pepper, matzo meal, and water. Combine well.

Fill a large pot half full with water. Add the fish heads, bones, salt, pepper, carrots, and onions, and bring to a rapid boil. When the water is boiling, form the ground fish mixture into round balls, using your hands. You can moisten your hands with water to make it easier to form the balls. Make each ball the size of a small apple (the yield should be about 12 balls).

Drop the fish balls into the rapidly boiling water. There should be enough water to cover the balls completely. Cover the pot and simmer for 2½ to 3 hours. When finished, remove the fish balls and continue to boil the remaining broth until it is reduced by half. Return the fish balls to the boiled down, strained broth, and refrigerate the fish balls and broth. If you've done everything correctly, the liquid should form a gel. Reheat the balls and broth before serving. Serves 10 to 12.

Lobster Vichyssoise

City Fish Market, Wethersfield, Connecticut

5 cups chicken stock

2 cups leeks, chopped

4 cups all-purpose potatoes, peeled and cut into ½-inch cubes

¼ teaspoon thyme

1 teaspoon black pepper

¼ teaspoon white wine Worcestershire sauce

2 cups all-purpose cream

2 teaspoons Dijon mustard

10–12 ounces fresh-picked lobster meat, cut into bite-size pieces

¼ cup parsley, chopped

¼ cup scallions, chopped

Vichyssoise is a cold potato soup that most likely originated in France (though Julia Child would beg to differ). Connecticut's City Fish Market has a recipe that calls for the addition of lobster, and the end result is a delightfully tasty, cold lobster soup with a French twist.

Bring the chicken stock to a boil in a stockpot. Add the leeks, potatoes, thyme, pepper, and Worcestershire sauce. Bring the mixture to a boil again, cover, and let it simmer for 1 hour.

Remove the pot from the heat and drain off 1 cup of the liquid. Purée the rest of the mixture a little at a time with a blender or food processor. Add the cream proportionally to each batch of the mixture that you purée. Add the mustard on the last batch.

Place the puréed soup in a container and add the lobster meat, mixing thoroughly.

Chill the soup for four hours or longer to allow the flavors to come together. Serve in chilled bowls, and top each serving with the chopped parsley and scallions. Serves 8.

Pinkham's Fish Chowder

Pinkham's Seafood, Boothbay, Maine

½ pound salt pork, sliced thin

1 medium-size yellow onion,
chopped fine

½ cup (1 stick) unsalted butter

5 pounds white potatoes, peeled
and cubed

2½ to 3 pounds whitefish fillets
(haddock or cod work best),
cut into large chunks

Salt and pepper

2 cans Carnation evaporated milk

1 quart whole milk

Using a large stock-pot or kettle, fry up the salt pork on low heat until the pork pieces are browned. Remove the pork scraps from the kettle, leaving the grease in the bottom of the pot. Add the diced onion and stick of butter. Cook on medium heat until the onions are almost transparent.

Add the potatoes and just enough water to cover them. Continue to cook on medium to high heat until the potatoes are slightly tender, approximately 10 minutes. Add chunks of fish and the salt and pepper. Cover the kettle to let the fish steam and the potatoes continue to cook for 10–15 minutes, or until the fish turns white and flakes easily with a fork. Stirring gently, add 2 cans of evaporated milk. Remove the pot from the heat, and add 1 quart of whole milk. Serves 10 to 12.

Tip: Chowder always seems to taste better after it sits for a day or overnight, but if you plan to cook and serve the same day, add 3 chicken bouillon cubes to the water when cooking up the potatoes. It adds a little extra stock/flavor.

STARTERS

Anthony's Seafood

Middletown, Rhode Island

Housed in a warehouse-like building on a commercial stretch of highway 138 (Aquidneck Avenue) in Middletown, Rhode Island, Anthony's is by far the best place to go for fresh seafood in the Newport and southeastern Rhode Island area. Owner Steve Bucolo, along with co-owner and brother Mike, run a tight ship and have one of the most amazing seafood display counters you'll see anywhere.

The Anthony's Seafood story begins on the docks of Newport in the 1950s. Founder Anthony Bucolo opened a wholesale lobster company on Spring Wharf, eventually expanding over the next thirty years into the wholesale fish and seafood production businesses. He also opened a retail fish market in the 1970s in the same location, and it was an immediate hit with the locals and tourists.

For a brief period in the 1980s, Anthony sold the business, which by that time had moved to Waite's Wharf and included a floating restaurant. A couple of years later, Bucolo bought the seafood business back and gave his sons a chance to take over the operation, which they continue to run to this day. In the late 1990s, Steve and Mike decided to move out of the high-rent downtown Newport business district and relocate their business several miles north in Middletown. They wanted to be nearer to their local, year-round customer base, and they've never regretted the move.

The glass-fronted seafood counter—which confronts you right when you walk through the front door—runs twenty-nine feet long, and is stocked with a wide variety of fresh seafood and prepared foods for carry out, all in stainless steel servers sitting atop huge beds of crushed ice. Check out the amazing variety of salmon fillets from New England, Canada, Scotland, and Alaska, many of them wild caught or organically grown. Local finned fish include the standard cod, haddock, swordfish, sole, and flounder, as well as sometimes harder to find items like monkfish, redfish, and halibut.

There is an equally wide variety of shellfish—medium, large, jumbo, and colossal shrimp, primarily from the Gulf of Mexico; several different types of oysters harvested from beds throughout New England; and clams of every known local variety.

As far as prepared foods go, right at the top of the list is Anthony's famous Portuguese Fish Chowder, with its thick, creamy texture and the distinctive spicy bite of its chouriço sausage (see the recipe on page 18). There's also an excellent stuffed lobster in the refrigerator cases, along with clams casino, oysters Rockefeller, scallops wrapped in bacon, seafood-stuffed mushrooms, stuffed jumbo shrimp, seafood-stuffed sole, and Anthony's equally famous stuffed quahogs, aka "stuffies," full of minced clams, bread stuffing, chouriço sausage, and spices, all packed into a large quahog shell (see the recipe on the next page).

Before or after you stock up on your seafood favorites at the market, you may wish to sit down for a meal in Anthony's adjacent dining room, an airy spot with a vaulted ceiling, booths, and tables where dining in the rough is the order of the day. There are also a few tables outside the front door to consider when the weather is nice. The menu boasts all the deep-fried seafoods you would expect to find in a seafood shack, along with boiled lobster, shore dinners, "stuffies," and a very unusual and highly popular kung pao calamari with hot peppers, plum chili sauce, peanuts, and scallions.

If you find yourself in the Newport area, looking for good, fresh seafood and a nice place to grab an affordable bite to eat, beat a path to Anthony's for all your New England seafood needs. There's also plenty of free parking—something not easily found down the road in Newport!

Stuffed Quahogs

Anthony's Seafood, Middletown, Rhode Island

10 large live quahog clams

1 stick butter

6 ounces ground or diced chouriço
    (Portuguese-smoked sausage)

4 ounces white onion, diced

3¼ ounces hot pepper relish

12 ounces plain croutons

1 ounce fresh parsley, chopped

2 to 6 ounces plain breadcrumbs

Also known in Rhode Island and elsewhere as "stuffies," this popular, spicy appetizer-type clam dish presents well and tastes great. This particular recipe calls for chouriço, a spicy Portuguese smoked sausage popular and readily available in the Portuguese maritime communities of Rhode Island and southeastern Massachusetts. If you can't find chouriço at your grocery store or butcher shop, Mexican chorizo sausage makes a reasonable substitute.

Preheat the oven to 400 degrees. In a medium pot, bring 4 cups of water to a boil over high heat. Place the quahogs in the pot and let them steam until they open, 5 to 6 minutes. Remove the quahogs, strain the water from the pot (which is now quahog broth), and reserve the broth for later use. Then remove the clam meat from the shells and, when cool, chop into chunky ¼-inch pieces, or use a food processor (don't over-process—the meat should be chunky). The shells may be set aside for later use. Make sure to remove any muscles left on the shells and discard any broken shells.

In a large skillet over medium-high heat, add the butter, chouriço, onions, and pepper relish, and cook until the onions become translucent. Add the chopped quahog meat, and cook for 3 to 4 minutes longer.

In a large mixing bowl, add the quahog broth to the croutons and fold together. When the croutons have absorbed the broth, add the hot ingredients to the bowl. Incorporate all of the ingredients, adding enough plain breadcrumbs until the mixture is stiff. Divide the mixture into 10 even balls, about 5 ounces each or 3 inches in diameter, and place them firmly into the quahog shells. Place the shells on a sheet pan and bake until the outside of the "stuffie" is toasted brown, 5 to 10 minutes. Serves 10 as appetizers or 5 (2 each) as a main course.

Salmon Pâté

Free Range Fish and Lobster, Portland, Maine

POACHING WATER

3 cups water

1 lemon slice

1 garlic clove

1 bay leaf

8 ounces salmon, skinned

¼ cup onion, diced

1–2 garlic cloves

⅓ cup parsley

2 tablespoons butter

4 ounces cream cheese, softened

¼ teaspoon salt

¼ teaspoon pepper

Try this homemade recipe for salmon pâté from Free Range Fish and Lobster, which sits next to the commercial docks in Portland, Maine. You may never go the store-bought pâté route again.

Using a baking dish, gently poach the salmon in the poaching water until flesh flakes easily.

While the fish is poaching, dice the onion, garlic, and parsley. Heat the butter until it is soft enough to mix with the cream cheese. In a large bowl, thoroughly combine the cream cheese, butter, parsley, onion, garlic, salt, and pepper. Add the poached salmon, and gently mix until smooth throughout. Yields 1⅓ pounds of pâté.

Jess's Market

Rockland, Maine

Jess's Market turns thirty in 2016, and there will be much to celebrate. The market is known as the best, most reliable place to get fresh fish in the tri-town area of Rockland, Rockport, and Camden, as well as the rest of the western shore of Penobscot Bay. In fact, many consider it to be the best place to get fresh fish north of Portland, Maine. In addition to their retail shop, Jess's supplies seafood to all the best restaurants between Belfast and Thomaston, and they even stock the occasional American Cruise Line ship that stops into Rockland Harbor on coastal Maine tours.

Owned and run by Sharon O'Brien, Jess's is a family operation, with daughters Lisa Gordon and Katie Wiggin constantly present at the market, helping their mother run things year-round. The market itself is a charming, airy room with two beautiful seafood cases, several refrigerator cases of prepared foods and craft beer, an alcove stocked with outstanding wines, shelves in the middle of the store that are laden with all sorts of gourmet foods, and a very large and active lobster tank. (Most of the red guys are in voluminous tanks in back. Jess's sells a lot of lobster wholesale throughout the region, in addition to their brisk retail lobster business.)

The lobsters at Jess's come almost exclusively from local sources—day boat lobstermen in the area and wharves where other lobstermen offload and sell their catches to retailers such as Jess's. With the cold, dark waters of Penobscot Bay and other mid-coast Maine bays and rivers close by, there's no lack of supply, except in winter, when Jess's buys its catch from the brave and hardy lobster fishermen of Monhegan Island, some of the few fishermen to pull traps during the harsh winter season.

Inside Jess's seafood cases are staples such as cod, haddock, flounder, Scottish salmon, squid from Rhode Island, and shrimp from Ecuador. Various types of clams and sea scallops are also available year-round, with scallops purchased directly from dragger boats on Penobscot Bay in wintertime.

What really makes Jess's stand out are the rare seafood items they bring in—things you can't get anywhere else this far north in Maine, such as shad roe from the Connecticut River, fresh soft-shell blue crabs from the Chesapeake Bay area, John Dory, black cod, and bay scallops from Cape Cod in winter. The market also has special connections to keep them supplied regularly with sometimes hard-to-find, fresh-picked Maine crabmeat of the peeky-toe and Jonah variety, among others. Sharon says that picking crabmeat in Maine is a dying art practiced by only a small group of knowledgeable old-timers (hopefully the skills will be passed along).

One final thing to consider before departing from this wonderful seafood emporium: Jess's has its own smoker out back where they smoke up salmon on a regular basis, along with haddock for Scottish finnan haddie and black cod when it's in season. This is the perfect place to pick up some fish, a lobster or two, and a nice bottle of wine, and enjoy a feast on the shores of Penobscot Bay.

Steamed Clams

Jess's Market, Rockland, Maine

2–4 pounds soft shell (steamer)
 clams

Water

Handful of salt

4 ounces (½ stick) melted butter

Here's a foolproof way to steam fresh clams on the stovetop or grill. Be sure to discard any broken clams before steaming.

Put the clams in a large pot. Cover them with water, and swish the clams around by hand to clean them. Drain the water and repeat the process until the water appears free of sand and grit.

Put about 1 inch of water in the bottom of the pot, along with the rinsed clams. Mix in the salt, turn the heat to high, and cover. Cook until the shells open, about 10 to 12 minutes. Carefully remove the clams with long-handled tongs, and serve with melted butter.

Tip: Retain the clam broth from the bottom of the pot and put it in cups on the table for rinsing the clams before dousing them in butter and eating them. Serves 2 to 4.

Mussels in Wine Sauce

City Fish Market, Wethersfield, Connecticut

4 pounds mussels, cleaned and de-bearded

4 tablespoons shallots, chopped

2 cloves garlic, chopped fine

1½ cups white wine

2 tablespoons butter

2 tablespoons fresh parsley, chopped

Salt and freshly ground pepper to taste

Davina Anagnos of City Fish Market recommends this quick and easy shellfish dish for a simple yet satisfying meal on Mother's Day. No muss, no fuss, and guaranteed to put a smile on any seafood-loving mother's face!

Place the mussels in a pot with the shallots, garlic, and white wine. Cover the pot and steam until the mussels open. Discard any mussels that remain closed after the steaming, then remove the cooked mussels and set them aside.

Reduce the remaining liquid in the pot by half over medium high heat. Add the butter, parsley, salt, and pepper. Pour the liquid over the cooked mussels and serve immediately. Serves 4.

Fritto Misto

New Deal Fish Market, Cambridge, Massachusetts

8 medium to small smelts or
   8 small whiting, scaled and
   gutted

8 medium squid and tentacles,
   cleaned and cut into small
   rings

16 medium or large shrimp
   (26/30 count per pound),
   peeled and de-veined

8 fresh sardines, scaled and gutted

8 small monkfish chunks, skinned
   and deboned

Frying oil (grapeseed/canola or
   canola mixed with olive oil
   works best)

All-purpose flour

Parsley (for garnishing)

Salt and pepper to taste

Lemon wedges (optional)

Fritto misto is an Italian term that translates as "mixed fry." The Italians typically use this term to refer to frying a variety of seafoods. In the home of New Deal Fish Market owner Carl Fantasia, it is tradition to have a seafood feast on Christmas Eve, and fritto misto is one of several courses served that evening. This recipe is very easy to prepare and can be served as an appetizer or a main course.

Begin by rinsing all the scaled, gutted, and cleaned seafood, then pat it dry to remove most of the water. Over medium-high heat in a large frying pan, heat the frying oil. There should be about ¼ inch or more of frying oil in the pan.

While the oil is heating, place some all-purpose flour in a bowl and put some of the seafood in the bowl. Coat each piece of seafood with the flour, shake off the excess, and place each piece carefully in the hot oil (you may need 2 frying pans to fry all seafood at once, depending on the size of your pans).

Fry the seafood on each side for 2–4 minutes, or until it's crisp and golden brown, and place it on a large dish/tray lined with 2 or 3 paper towels to absorb the excess oil. Remove the paper towels or transfer the fried seafood onto a serving tray, garnish with parsley, season with salt and pepper, and serve immediately. Serves 4 as a main course, 6 as an appetizer.

Tip: This dish should be served warm/hot and should never be covered and left for later. Covering the warm seafood will make it soggy, not crispy. Lemon may be squeezed on the seafood prior to serving.

Mac's Seafood Market

Wellfleet, Massachusetts

If ever there were a seafood market worthy of being called an empire, Mac's would be it. With four outstanding retail markets on the outer reaches of Cape Cod (one each in Provincetown, Wellfleet, Truro, and Eastham) and three restaurants (one in Provincetown, two in Wellfleet), Mac's truly has the Outer Cape waterfront covered. Yet, despite its size, Mac's is one of the most considerate and benevolent fish operations in New England, with one-on-one relationships with local fishing families that go back to the Market's founding.

Macgregor "Mac" Hay and his brother Alex got the ball rolling in 1995, when they took over a modest seafood market in the rear of a shingled, 1½-story building next to the town pier in Wellfleet. A seafood shack occupied the front portion.

The Hays' dedication to purchasing, selling, and promoting the wonderful fish and shellfish from nearby waters set them apart from many of the larger markets on the Cape that shopped far and wide for the best deals they could get from large wholesalers. The Hays preferred to buy from the local fishing families, something they practice to this day.

It wasn't long before Mac's had a solid following in the northern reaches of the Cape. Eventually the brothers purchased the seafood shack in the front of the building and renamed it Mac's Seafood. Mac had a culinary background and at that time spent his winters cooking at establishments in Boston and New York.

The brothers kept their thriving seafood market in the

back, with its separate entrance on the side of the building. It's a beautiful place within—a large table of ice, covered with the freshest fillets, whole fish, and shellfish you'll find anywhere. Virtually every ID sign in the display case begins with the word "local."

Given the market's prime location on the docks in Wellfleet, it's no surprise that one of Mac's signature products is Wellfleet oysters. The fabled shellfish have prospered in Wellfleet harbor's shallow, calm waters for hundreds of years. Renowned for their fresh, briny flavor and for their round and plump dimensions, these freshly shucked beauties are excellent raw, warmed, or smoked in their half shells on the grill.

Finned fish are always plentiful at all four markets, the most popular being cod, haddock, halibut, flounder, pollock, monkfish, tuna, swordfish, and salmon. These fillets are ideal for baking in the oven, frying in the pan, or charring on the grill. Most are of local origin, and most are available year-round.

Smoked fish are another Mac's specialty, with each of the four markets smoking its own fish on the premises. The two varieties most frequently smoked are salmon and bluefish. Mac's also makes its own smoked salmon pâté and smoked bluefish pâté, both available in the refrigerated cases alongside the gourmet cheeses and pre-made clam chowder.

Lobsters are a mainstay at Mac's, with several lobster boats dedicated to fishing for the retailer. Mac's catches come from the "back shore" (the Atlantic side of the Upper Cape, where the water is deeper and colder and better for propagating large, tasty lobsters). If you wish, any of the markets will be happy to cook your take-away lobsters for free and save you the hassle of cooking them yourself. Each of the shacks also carries a limited line of fine meats and other gourmet items.

"Sustainable" and "locally harvested" are well-worn buzzwords these days in the food business, but they've been a way of life at Mac's from the beginning. About the only seafood that comes from afar are the Pacific salmon and the Mexican shrimp. Even in these instances, the Hays have direct relationships with the fishermen, which enables them to live by their creed of keeping their business personal, local, and sustainable. This makes all the difference in the quality of their seafood, and explains why Mac's has met with so much success in its twenty years and counting on the Cape.

Striped Bass Crudo

Mac's Seafood, Wellfleet, Massachusetts

½ pound fresh striped bass fillet (preferably the thicker head cut), skinned

1 tablespoon fresh lime juice (about ½ lime)

Pinch of coarse sea salt

Freshly cracked black pepper

2 tablespoons top-shelf extra virgin olive oil

A few drops of Sriracha (Thai-style hot sauce; the Huy Fong "Rooster" brand is recommended)

This chilled appetizer is perfect for those too-hot-to-cook days that mark the beginning of the local striped bass season on Cape Cod and elsewhere. Though "crudo" means "raw" in Italian, the citrus juice in this recipe does make the fish opaque and firmer in texture. This recipe from Mac's Seafood calls for lime and Thai hot sauce, where Italians might prefer lemon and basil. Either way, high-quality, fresh olive oil is key. (Special thanks goes to Elspeth Hay, author of the blog "Diary of a Locavore," for perfecting this recipe.)

Slice the bass fillet lengthwise, across the grain of the fish, into thin strips. Arrange the strips so that they overlap just slightly to form several lines across a large, chilled plate. Cover tightly with plastic wrap, and press the strips firmly with the bottom of a cup to flatten the fish. Put the plated fish in the refrigerator for up to several hours, and pull it out just before you're ready to serve. (It's best to dress the fish just before serving. Marinating the fish in citrus juices for longer would make this delicate crudo taste a little overdone.)

Remove the plastic wrap, then pour the lime juice over the fish and sprinkle it with sea salt and cracked pepper. Drizzle the olive oil over the top, and dot the rim of the plate with the Sriracha, to serve as a dipping sauce. Serve at once. Serves 4.

Hot 'n' Spicy Crab Dip

Free Range Fish and Lobster, Portland, Maine

2 roasted jalapeño peppers

2 garlic cloves, diced

½ onion, diced

⅓ cup mayonnaise

½ cup Parmesan cheese

8 ounces cream cheese, softened

2 tablespoons Melinda's Extra
   Hot Habañero Sauce (or
   equivalent)

2 tablespoons hot pepper sauce

½ teaspoon cayenne pepper

Juice of ½ lemon

1 pound crabmeat, cooked

Preheat the oven to 400 degrees.

Roast the whole jalapeños until they're *al dente*, about 3–4 minutes, and allow them to cool down. Devein and deseed the jalapeños, and dice with the garlic and onion.

In a bowl, mix the diced vegetables with the mayonnaise, Parmesan cheese, cream cheese, hot sauces, cayenne pepper, and lemon juice. Add the crabmeat and mix everything thoroughly.

Bake in an oven-safe dish for 6–8 minutes or until it's bubbling. Alternatively, you may heat the mixture in a double boiler until the dip is hot. Yields 2 pounds of dip, enough for an appetizer for 12 people.

Baked Mussels

Port Lobster Company, Kennebunkport, Maine

2 pounds mussels, cleaned and
    with beards removed

3 garlic cloves, coarsely chopped

1 cup fresh flat-leaf parsley,
    chopped

4 tablespoons (½ stick) unsalted
    butter, cut into several chunks

¼ teaspoon salt

¼ teaspoon black pepper

This is a wonderful way to prepare mussels for either an appetizer or a main course. It's simple, and because it cooks up in the oven, your stovetop should be spared the muss and fuss usually associated with steaming mussels in messy, boiling pots.

Preheat the oven to 450 degrees. Spread the mussels in a 9 × 13-inch baking dish. Blend all the remaining ingredients to a paste in a food processor, and spoon the mixture over the mussels.

Cover the baking dish tightly with foil and bake on the middle oven rack until the mussels open, about 12 to 15 minutes. Discard any unopened mussels. Serves 4 for an appetizer or 2 for a main course.

Chatham Pier Fish Market

Chatham, Massachusetts

This is one of the few remaining fish markets in New England (or anywhere, for that matter) where one can actually watch commercial fishing boats pull up to the dock and offload their fresh catch, a practice that for the most part has been relegated to the larger, less accessible fishing ports in places like New Bedford and Boston, Massachusetts, and Portland, Maine.

It's quite a sight to see hundreds of fish hoisted up from the decks and then dumped onto stainless steel slides. At the bottom of the slides are large, wheeled containers that transport the catch to the dock warehouse for processing and shipment, or for sale in the fish market next door. Nearly a hundred day boats service Chatham Pier, and you'll see them queuing up in the cove to offload their catches, especially in the afternoon.

The grey-shingled fish market and pier is located on Aunt Lydia's Cove, a very scenic and popular part of Cape Cod—right at the elbow of the Cape, where the landmass stops its eastward progression and juts straight north toward Provincetown. There are basically two parts to the fish market operation: one part is a cozy, modest market with fresh fish and shellfish on display, and the other is a dine-in-the-rough eatery with a simple yet satisfying menu of mostly deep-fried seafood items and a killer lobster roll. Let's take a look at the retail market first.

The interior of the fish market is illuminated with old-fashioned fluorescent-tube lighting hung from the exposed rafters that support the pitched roof of the Cape-style building. The fluorescent glow gives the place a homey, retro feel. The ice-filled fresh-fish case is stocked with the catches of the day, such as cod, haddock, scallops, dogfish, skate, bluefish, halibut, flounder, and locally harvested clams and mussels. The fish are hand-cut in the kitchen by experienced workers, so the fillets are as fresh as can be. There's also a large lobster tank, where you may select your own lobsters to take home or

to have cooked up by the cook staff on the premises. It's likely that what you see in the seafood case was swimming not far offshore earlier that day.

If you plan to dine on the pier, you'll order your food inside the market and pick it up outside through a window on the side of the building. The fried clams and fish and chips are popular items, and the lobster roll (chilled, with a bit of mayo) is one of the largest, freshest, and finest on the Cape. Be fore-warned that there are no tables inside or outside the market. Many people sit along a bench stretching across the rear of the market building overlooking the harbor, or they use the hoods of their cars as impromptu dining room tables.

Regardless of whether you're buying fresh fish to cook at home (or your vacation rental) or you prefer to partake of the deep-fried goodies from the shack, Chatham Pier Fish Market is a delightful place to witness a working fish pier in operation and have some excellent seafood at the same time.

Smoked Fish Pâté

Chatham Pier Fish Market, Chatham, Massachusetts

1½ pounds cream cheese, softened

1½ pounds smoked fish (bluefish, salmon, and trout are good choices)

⅛ cup lemon juice

½ cup mayonnaise

½ tablespoon Tabasco sauce

¼ cup horseradish

½ tablespoon black pepper

¼ cup parsley

Why pay high prices for fancy pâté when you can make your own at home with some smoked fish from your local seafood market? This recipe calls for a large party bowl of pâté, but you may always reduce each ingredient and make a smaller batch.

Soften the cream cheese by leaving it out at room temperature for an hour or two.

Place the softened cream cheese into a large bowl. Break or chop the smoked fish into small, bite-size pieces, and place the pieces in the bowl with the cream cheese. Add the lemon juice, mayonnaise, Tabasco, horseradish, black pepper, and parsley, and mix well. Refrigerate the mixture for at least two hours to allow the flavors to come together. Transfer to a serving dish, and serve at room temperature for best flavor. Serves 12.

Cold Crabmeat Dip

Trenton Bridge Lobster Pound, Trenton, Maine

1 8-ounce package cream cheese

2 tablespoons onion, chopped

2 tablespoons ketchup

¼ teaspoon Worcestershire sauce

½ teaspoon salt

2 tablespoons cream or half-and-
half creamer

2 tablespoons mayonnaise

1 pound crabmeat

This crab dip recipe is about as basic as it gets, but if you use fresh-picked crabmeat, this dip more than holds its own when put up against more complicated recipes.

Blend well after adding each ingredient. Mix with electric mixer until smooth. Serve with crackers or chopped raw vegetables, such as carrot sticks, celery, or broccoli florets. Serves 6 as an appetizer.

SALADS

Seared Scallop Salad

Bayley's Lobster Pound, Scarborough, Maine

½ pound fresh sea scallops

½ cup olive oil, plus 1 teaspoon

3 tablespoons white wine vinegar

1 tablespoon mayonnaise

1 teaspoon Dijon mustard

Salt and pepper

1 garlic clove, smashed

Mixed greens

½ red bell pepper, seeded and cut into strips

½ yellow bell pepper, seeded and cut into strips

This light and refreshing salad from Bayley's Lobster Pound in Maine is perfect for a summertime lunch or dinner. It's easy to make and a very diet-friendly choice that's also full of nutrition.

Rinse the sea scallops and pat them dry with a towel. Toss the scallops with 1 teaspoon of olive oil. Heat a skillet over medium high heat until very hot. Pour in the olive oil and heat until it just begins to smoke. Carefully place each scallop in the pan with the flat sides down. Cook for 1½ minutes per side, flipping them once gently with tongs.

In a small bowl, whisk together the vinegar, mayonnaise, mustard, salt, pepper, and garlic. Slowly whisk in the olive oil in a stream. Combine the mixed greens and bell pepper strips in a large bowl. When the scallops are done, toss the dressing with the greens. Arrange the scallops on top of the greens and bell pepper strips. Serves 2.

Star Fish Market

Guilford, Connecticut

Tucked away in a courtyard-shaped strip mall on the Boston Post Road (U.S. 1) in Guilford, Connecticut, is the Star Fish Market, a bright, cheery retailer that's been a favorite of shoreline seafood shoppers for the past couple of decades. With its stark white walls, black-and-white-checkered pillars, and white ceramic tile floor, it's always bright and cheerful looking inside, even on the gloomiest of days.

Star Fish Market owners Mike and Collette Lukas pride themselves in procuring the freshest seafood possible for their customers. Each day, they seek out a variety of at least twenty fresh fish and shellfish varieties, many of them seasonal, from their suppliers. They display their products in an alluring fashion, showing only small samples of each in their constantly changing, artfully designed display cases. The bulk of the inventory resides in a much cooler refrigerator in back, guaranteeing super fresh seafood with each order.

The Lukases work hard to ensure that they get the best of the catch from their wholesalers and that the fish and shellfish they purchase are all caught in an environmentally friendly and sustainable manner. This is not a high-volume operation but rather a boutique seafood market that emphasizes quality and a lot of personal, attentive service—an imperative, given the market's upscale location.

Another hallmark of this shoreline gem is the variety of its prepared foods and its sidelines of gourmet cheeses, breads, and meats. Salad offerings tend toward the healthy, such as shrimp and couscous salad, poached salmon salad, seaweed salad, and

edamame. Homemade chowders and bisques are available in containers in the store's refrigerator and freezer cases. There are also several shelves full of gourmet grocery items, such as a variety of olive oils, pastas, and numerous jars and cans of exotic ingredients and spices from around the world.

Keep this award-winning seafood market in mind if you're vacationing along the Connecticut shoreline. The Lukases and their cheerful, helpful staff will make sure you leave with a smile on your face and some great seafood and other goodies in your basket.

Shrimp and Israeli Couscous Salad

Star Fish Market, Guilford, Connecticut

1¼ pounds large (26–30 count) raw shrimp, peeled and deveined, no tails

1¼ cups water

1 cup uncooked Israeli couscous

6 ounces sundried tomatoes

1 cucumber

15 ounces mandarin orange slices

2 tablespoons vegetable oil

Salt and pepper, to taste

6 sprigs cilantro, diced

This is an excellent salad for the summertime. It's filled with lots of different, complementary flavors and plenty of healthy ingredients.

Steam or boil the shrimp for 1½ minutes. Cool them in cold water or ice for 3–4 minutes, drain, and set aside.

In a heavy pot, heat the water to boiling. Add the couscous, turn the heat down to a simmer, and cover the pot, continuing to simmer for 8 minutes. Stir once after 4 minutes.

In a large bowl combine the cooked couscous and shrimp. Dice the sundried tomatoes, reserving the juice, then add the diced tomatoes and juice to the couscous and shrimp. Scrape the seeds from the cucumber, then dice the cucumber and add it to the bowl. Add the mandarin orange slices to the bowl, along with a little of the juice from the oranges. Pour in the vegetable oil, then salt and pepper to taste and the diced cilantro. Mix gently and serve. Serves 6.

Poached Salmon Salad with Leeks and Shallots

Star Fish Market, Guilford, Connecticut

1½ pounds sashimi-grade, organic-fed salmon

1½ tablespoons extra-virgin olive oil

3 shallots, diced

½ pound leeks, white sections only, diced

2 tablespoons tarragon, chopped

3 tablespoons mayonnaise

2 tablespoons mascarpone

Salt and pepper to taste

This rich, creamy salmon salad is best with the sashimi-grade, organically fed salmon that Star Fish Market recommends in the recipe, but it also works very well with other grades and even with leftover salmon from the oven or grill.

Prep the salmon so that you have 1½ pounds of salmon meat after it has been skinned and had the dark meat removed (you may want to have your seafood market do this for you). Poach the salmon in water for 7 minutes, or shorter if the fillet is thin. The salmon should be ¾ cooked when removed from the water—still firm and not flaky. Set it aside, and let the fish drain in a colander over a sink or paper towels.

Coat a sauté pan with a thin layer of olive oil, and warm under medium heat. Add the diced shallots and the diced white sections of the leeks, then simmer for 20 minutes, stirring periodically.

Place the poached salmon, shallots, and leeks in a large bowl. Add the chopped tarragon. Mix the mayonnaise and mascarpone together in a separate bowl, then blend it in with the salmon and other ingredients. Salt and pepper to taste, then serve at room temperature. Serves 6.

Thai-Style Squid Salad

City Fish Market, Wethersfield, Connecticut

½ cup fresh lime juice

1 tablespoon sugar

1 tablespoon fresh ginger, peeled
    and minced

1½ teaspoons salt

1 red or yellow bell pepper, cut into
    thin strips

½ cup scallions, thinly sliced

1 small hot chili, minced (see Tip)
    or ¼ teaspoon red pepper
    flakes

¼ cup fresh mint, chopped

¼ cup fresh cilantro, chopped

¼ cup fresh basil, chopped

1 pound squid sacs and tentacles,
    cleaned

The fresh, light flavors of ginger, lime, and herbs make this fat-free salad sparkle on the tongue. Serve it as an appetizer or turn it into a room-temperature main course by tossing it with thin, cooked noodles.

In a salad bowl, stir together the lime juice, sugar, ginger, salt, and 3 tablespoons water. Add the bell pepper, scallions, chili, mint, cilantro, and basil.

Cut the squid sacs into ¼-inch rings and halve the tentacles. In a saucepan of boiling salted water, cook the squid for 1 minute, until it's opaque and tender (overcooking as little as 30 seconds will toughen the squid). Drain immediately and add to the herb mixture.

Toss the salad and let it stand for 30 minutes at room temperature before serving. The salad can be kept, chilled and covered, up to two days. Serves 4 as a main course or 6 as a salad.

Tip: A small, thin red Thai chili may be used in this salad, but a Serrano or jalapeno is a good substitute. Beware that most of the heat in a chili is in the seeds and varies in intensity from chili to chili. Mince a whole chili, seeds and all, and add a little bit at a time until the salad has reached the desired spiciness.

Port Clyde Fresh Catch Fish Cooperative

Port Clyde, Maine

The Port Clyde Fish Cooperative is about as informal as fish markets get. Housed in a one-story warehouse-like building just off the docks of Port Clyde, there is no marketplace to speak of. You enter through the front door of the warehouse into a somewhat disheveled office space where there is an ancient telephone intercom device on the desk with a note attached to it that reads: PLEASE PRESS BUTTON FOR SERVICE. Once pressed, a fisherman eventually emerges from the recesses of the warehouse, ready to tell you what sort of fresh catch they have on hand that day. No display cases, no burbling tanks or seductive prepared-food refrigerators—just good, old-fashioned fish and shellfish fresh off the boat.

The cooperative was founded in 2008 by about a dozen local fishermen who were being slowly squeezed out of their livelihood by increasingly strict regulations, diminishing fish stocks in the Gulf of Maine, and competition from bigger fishing vessels, large wholesalers, and international seafood conglomerates. Taking a page from the local agriculture movement playbook, the fishermen decided to effectively cut out the middlemen and sell direct to local seafood markets, grocery stores, restaurants—and to individuals who sign up on a subscription basis to receive whatever the fresh catch

of the day or week may be throughout the fishing season. It hasn't been a wild success, but the cooperative is still chugging along, keeping the fishermen happy and in business, doing what they love.

Typical offerings at the cooperative include fresh-picked crabmeat (many of the cooperative members spend their shore time in the warehouse, picking), grey sole, flounder, redfish, hake, haddock, pollock, and cod. Frozen items include fish pieces for chowder and frozen versions of most of the finned fish previously mentioned. The cooperative used to be a main port of entry for boats catching Maine shrimp in the wintertime, but fishing for the small, sweet delicacies has been suspended due to a severe collapse of the fishery. Keep your fingers crossed that the little pink shrimp make a comeback, as they're delightfully sweet and may be served in myriad ways, fresh or frozen.

Port Clyde Fresh Catch is a noble cause with a big payback: some of the freshest fish you'll find anywhere along the coast of Maine. So, step into the office, hit that intercom button, and tell the guys you're ready to buy some of their catch. They'll benefit, and so will you.

Fish Salad

Port Clyde Fresh Catch, Port Clyde, Maine

2 cups fish, cooked

1 stalk celery, diced

1 tablespoon capers (optional)

2 tablespoons mayonnaise

1 tablespoon lemon juice

Salt and pepper to taste

Here's a great way to make good use of leftover fish in a tasty and healthy manner. Think lobster salad, only with fish. Makes sense, doesn't it?

Mix the ingredients together, and let them sit for at least 15 minutes to allow the flavors to come together. Serve on a toasted bagel or in a toasted split-top bun, as part of a salad plate, or wrapped in a flour tortilla with lettuce and tomato. Serves 2 to 3.

Barbara Bush's Favorite Lobster Salad

Clam Shack Seafood Market, Kennebunk, Maine

6 1-pound Maine lobsters

2 red bell peppers, halved and seeded

1 head of romaine

1 bunch fresh spinach

1 bag mixed greens

4 ounces feta cheese, diced

12 Kalamata olives, pitted

4 tablespoons pine nuts

High-quality French dressing (Crane Crest Real French Dressing works best)

This lobster salad has become the George H. W. Bush family's go-to healthy lunch choice when they are entertaining on Walker's Point in Kennebunkport. It has evolved from family chef Ariel Guzman's original version to the Bush family's current chef's rendition, which reflects ingredients from Greek cuisine. The Bush kitchen puts the salad together, and Clam Shack Seafood supplies the specially picked and separated lobster. Simple, delicious, and attractive, with the lobster arranged anatomically, it's a dramatic and elegant presentation that's also become a favorite in the home of Clam Shack owner Steve Kingston.

Cook the lobsters in rapidly boiling saltwater for 15 minutes. Cool, shuck, and separate the knuckles, tails, and claws. Arrange each lobster anatomically.

While the lobsters boil, preheat the broiler and broil the bell peppers, cut side down, until blackened. Remove the peppers from the oven and put them immediately into a paper bag to trap the steam. When cool, remove the skins from the peppers, and slice them thin.

In a large bowl, pile the washed and dried greens, the feta cheese, olives, pine nuts, and peppers.

Toss with the dressing. Top the salad with the anatomically arranged pieces of lobster meat. Serves 6.

Carolina Cole Slaw

Atlantic Seafood, Old Saybrook, Connecticut

COLE SLAW

1 pound shredded cabbage

½ pound shredded carrots

1 green bell pepper, sliced thin

1 red bell pepper, sliced thin

1 small sweet onion, sliced thin

DRESSING

½ cup olive oil

1 cup cider vinegar

2 teaspoons celery seed

2 teaspoons salt

2 teaspoons dry mustard

1 cup sugar

This colorful Carolina slaw comes by way of Jerry Doran of Atlantic Seafood on the Connecticut shoreline. It makes a great side dish with grilled fish, pulled pork sandwiches, and any sort of barbecue, especially in the summertime.

To make the cole slaw, mix the ingredients together and set aside.

For the slaw dressing, mix together all ingredients in a small pot. Bring it to a boil, then pour it over the shredded, sliced vegetables. Mix the vegetables and dressing until the vegetables are thoroughly coated. Cool in the refrigerator for at least an hour, to let the flavors come together. Makes 8 to 10 servings.

Hatch's Fish Market

Wellfleet, Massachusetts

Hatch's Fish Market is living proof that good things often come in small packages. This petite fish market and its adjoining produce stand are tucked away behind the old town hall in Wellfleet, Massachusetts, next to a municipal parking lot. With its wood-framed seafood display cases and its cozy, cheek-by-jowl sales floor (there's sometimes a line of people in the parking lot waiting to get inside), Hatch's is redolent of the fish markets of yore, when every small coastal New England town had one.

Cliff Hatch began his career like lots of New England fishmongers—selling fresh fish door-to-door from the back of his pickup truck. In 1954, Hatch built a small store in back of Wellfleet's town hall and began selling his fresh catch along with locally procured shellfish (including world-famous Wellfleet oysters), lobsters, and a small line of seafood accompaniments. It quickly became the place everyone in Wellfleet went for fresh fish. Starting out as a seasonal market, Hatch's remains so to this day, opening in mid-May and closing in mid-September.

Today, Hatch's wears two hats. It's still a wonderful seafood market in front, and the back half has been transformed into an impressive produce stand that's stocked with lots of locally sourced, in-season fruits and vegetables—almost like a farmer's market that's open every day in the summertime.

Current owner Adrien Kmiec still gets most of Hatch's seafood from the day boats that ply the waters of the outer Cape and deliver their goods to Wellfleet, Provincetown, and Chatham. Among the regularly stocked items are bluefish, cod, flounder, haddock, halibut, monkfish, pollock, and hake. Tuna and salmon (farm-raised and wild) are available most of the time, also. Shellfish include steamers, mussels, oysters (Wellfleet and otherwise), littlenecks, cherrystones, quahogs, and live lobsters.

Hatch's has been smoking its own fish and shellfish for over twenty years. First they brine and dry the fish, then smoke it for several hours in their own smoker. There's an extraordinary selection: bluefish, pollock, cod, salmon, haddock, scallops, halibut, striped bass, mackerel, swordfish, monkfish, and tuna—a far bigger lineup than just about any fish market anywhere in New England.

On most days, you can see Adrien and his crew filleting fish through the back door in the cutting room, a sure sign that the fish here is as fresh as can be. Check this place out the next time you're in Wellfleet, and pick up some fish and fresh veggies for a meal that will be as healthy, fresh, and tasty as any you'll find anywhere on the Cape.

PASTA

Pasta Primavera with Shrimp

Port Lobster Company, Kennebunkport, Maine

8 ounces ziti pasta

12 spears asparagus, cut into
2-inch lengths

1 16-ounce jar fresh mild salsa

4 ounces soft goat cheese

1 teaspoon sugar

½ pound cooked large shrimp

"Primavera" is a bit of a misnomer here, as this isn't strictly a vegetable-based dish. Nonetheless, this pasta recipe, combining shrimp, goat cheese, salsa, and asparagus, is unique and full of wonderful contradictions. This dish may be served hot, or it may be chilled and served as a cold pasta salad dish.

Cook the pasta in boiling water according to the label directions. Add the chopped asparagus to the boiling water during the last 5 minutes of cooking time. Drain the pasta and asparagus and set them aside.

In a large skillet over medium heat, heat the salsa, stirring frequently until the tomatoes release their juices, about 2 to 3 minutes. Stir in the goat cheese and sugar and heat until smooth. Add the cooked shrimp, and fold it in gently until heated through, about 2 minutes. Pour the sauce over the pasta and asparagus. Serves 4.

Tip: Before draining the pasta, dip out a cupful of the cooking water. If the pasta seems dry after it's been mixed with the sauce, add a little of the cooking water to moisten it.

Seafood Fra Diavolo

Bayley's Lobster Pound, Scarborough, Maine

1 pound linguine or other uncooked, spaghetti-like pasta

½ pound large raw shrimp, peeled and deveined

3 tablespoons olive oil, plus 1 to 2 tablespoons

1 teaspoon dried crushed red pepper flakes

1 medium onion, sliced

1 14½-ounce can diced tomatoes, including liquid

1 cup dry white wine

3 garlic cloves, chopped

¼ teaspoon dried oregano leaves

½ pound lobster meat

3 tablespoon fresh Italian parsley leaves, chopped

3 tablespoon fresh basil leaves, chopped

Salt to taste

Fra diavolo, which translates to "brother devil," is a popular pasta sauce in parts of New England and may be found on the menus of numerous seafood shacks and restaurants. The "devil" moniker stems from the crushed red pepper flakes that give the sauce its heat. There are many variations on the recipe, and this one from Bayley's Lobster Pound calls for plenty of shrimp and fresh lobster, along with the standard lineup of Italian herbs and spices.

Set a large pot of salted water to boil, and cook the pasta according to the instructions on the package.

While the water is heating up and the pasta is cooking, toss the shrimp in a medium bowl with 1 tablespoon of olive oil and the red pepper flakes. Heat the 2 tablespoons of olive oil in a large, heavy skillet over medium-high heat. Add the shrimp and sauté for about a minute, toss, and continue cooking until just cooked through, about 1 to 2 minutes. Transfer the shrimp to a large plate; set aside.

Add the onion to the same skillet, adding 1 to 2 teaspoons of olive oil to the pan, if necessary, and sauté until translucent, about 5 minutes. Add the can of tomatoes and liquid, wine, garlic, and oregano. Simmer until the sauce thickens slightly, about 10 minutes.

Add the lobster meat, and return the shrimp and any accumulated juices to the pan. Toss to coat the seafood, and cook for about a minute longer. Stir in the parsley and basil. Season with salt to taste. Serve over the pasta with warm, crusty bread and a simple salad on the side. Serves 4.

Linguine with Littleneck Clams and Genoa Salami

City Fish Market, Wethersfield, Connecticut

¾ pound linguine

3 tablespoons extra-virgin olive oil

2 garlic cloves, thinly sliced

¼ teaspoon crushed red pepper

30 littleneck clams, scrubbed

½ cup dry white wine

½ cup bottled clam broth

3 ounces sliced Genoa salami, cut into ½-inch strips

½ cup flat-leaf parsley leaves, coarsely chopped

This traditional New England Italian-American dish goes all out in terms of flavor with its fresh clams and strips of sliced Genoa salami blended into the pasta sauce.

Bring a large pot of salted water to a boil. Add the linguine and cook until it is *al dente*. Drain the linguine.

Meanwhile, in a large, deep skillet, heat the olive oil. Add the garlic and cook over moderate heat until lightly golden, about 3 minutes. Add the crushed red pepper, clams, and wine and bring to a boil. Add the clam broth, cover, and cook over moderate heat until the clams open, about 5 minutes. (Remove any clams that don't open.)

Add the linguine, salami, and parsley to the clam sauce, and toss over low heat until combined. Transfer the linguine mix to shallow bowls and serve immediately. Serves 3 to 4.

Tip: Serve with crusty bread to sop up the flavorful sauce left in each bowl.

Red Clam Sauce with Pasta

The Friendly Fisherman, North Eastham, Massachusetts

2–3 tablespoons olive oil

1–2 large cloves garlic, minced

2 tablespoons oregano, chopped (dried is fine, but fresh is best)

2 tablespoons basil, chopped

2 tablespoons parsley, chopped

9–10 fresh quahog clams (or 1 pint minced clams)

1 cup clam broth

1 29-ounce can crushed tomatoes, or equivalent freshly diced

1 5-ounce can tomato paste

1 pound linguine or thin spaghetti

1 cup Romano cheese, grated

Here's a simple clam sauce recipe from the humble, charming Friendly Fisherman seafood market and shack on the highway to Wellfleet and Provincetown. At its simplest, this sauce may be served straight up with pasta. It also makes a great base for bolder versions of seafood pasta as well. Just add whatever else you like—shrimp, fish, scallops, lobster—and enjoy a seafood-packed bowl of pasta!

In a large pot over medium heat, heat the olive oil, then add the garlic and herbs. Turn the heat down and simmer until the garlic is softened but not burned.

To prepare the sauce using quahogs, steam them open in a covered pot with two cups or so of water in the bottom, and reserve the water (this is now your clam broth). Shuck the clams and mince the meat in a food processor. If you're using minced clams, add them to the pot with the simmering garlic and herbs, along with the cup of clam juice. Add the tomatoes and tomato paste, and let it all simmer slowly for at least one hour.

Near the end of the simmering, bring a large pot of water to boil, and cook the pasta *al dente*, then strain and divide into serving bowls. Ladle the sauce on top of each serving, and sprinkle each with the Romano cheese. Serves 5 to 6.

Tips: Crushed red pepper flakes go great on top of this. You may also add more or less broth to make the clam sauce thicker or thinner.

Welcome To Jess's
Lobsters, Shellfish, Local Seafood,
Specialty Items, Fine Wines & Brews
Local Family Owned & Operated

Jess's Seafood Sauté

Jess's Market, Rockland, Maine

1 pound uncooked pasta

2 ounces whole anchovies

Red pepper flakes, to taste

2 tablespoons olive oil

Shrimp, squid, scallops, or clams
(allow 4 to 6 ounces per
serving)

¼ cup dry white wine

29 ounces tomatoes, diced, with
liquid

2 tablespoons fresh or dried
parsley flakes

Parmesan cheese

This sauté makes a great sauce with linguine-type pasta. Try it with any individual or combination of shellfish of your choosing.

Cook 1 pound of pasta in boiling water, according to the instructions on the packaging.

While the pasta is cooking, heat the anchovies and red pepper flakes in a skillet with the olive oil over medium heat until the anchovies fall apart. Add the seafood and sauté until opaque. Add the white wine and cook about 2 minutes. Add the diced tomatoes, continuing to stir. Garnish with parsley and serve over pasta. Sprinkle with Parmesan cheese, if desired. Serves 4 to 6.

Lobster Fettuccine Alfredo

Bayley's Lobster Pound, Scarborough, Maine

12 ounces dried egg fettuccine

½ cup (1 stick) plus 1 tablespoon unsalted butter

⅔ cup heavy cream

½ cup Parmigiano-Reggiano cheese, grated

1 pound lobster meat, cooked and cut into bite-size pieces

¼ teaspoon salt

¼ teaspoon black pepper

Fresh basil for garnish (optional)

This heavily lobster-laden pasta dish is a good one for when you crave lobster in the wintertime. It combines all the flavors of the sea with a calorie-heavy cream sauce and pasta—just what you need to combat the long, cold nights of winter.

Cook the pasta until *al dente* and drain. Reserve ½ cup of the cooking liquid.

While the pasta is cooking, melt the butter in a skillet over low heat. Add the heavy cream and bring the heat up to medium so that the mixture boils. Simmer and reduce the cream mixture a bit (about 5 minutes).

Put the drained pasta back into the pot in which it was cooked, and turn the heat up to medium high. Add the cream mixture to the pasta along with the Parmigiano-Reggiano and lobster meat and stir together. Add reserved cooking liquid to taste, if desired. Salt and pepper to taste, and garnish with fresh basil or additional Parmigiano. Serves 5 to 6.

Shrimp Scampi with Artichokes

Kyler's Catch Seafood Market, New Bedford, Massachusetts

1 pound uncooked pasta

2 tablespoons olive oil

1 small onion, sliced thin

1 tablespoon garlic, minced

1 pound raw jumbo shrimp, peeled and deveined

1 jar artichoke hearts, drained and quartered

⅓ cup white wine

1 teaspoon fresh lemon juice

Pinch of salt and pepper

2 tablespoons fresh parsley, chopped

Shrimp and artichoke hearts aren't exactly native to New England, but this winning pasta dish from Kyler's Catch borrows nicely from the Gulf Coast and the West Coast in a winning combination pasta dish.

Cook the pasta in a pot of boiling, salted water until *al dente*.

At the same time, heat the olive oil in a skillet over medium heat. Add the onions and garlic and cook for 2 to 3 minutes. Add the shrimp and artichokes, then the rest of the ingredients. Cook, stirring frequently, for 5 to 7 minutes, until the shrimp become opaque. Drain the pasta, and serve the shrimp/artichoke mixture over the pasta. Serves 5 to 6.

Superior Seafood

Westport, Connecticut

Tucked away in the Stiles Market on U.S. 1 in upscale Westport, Connecticut, Superior Seafood isn't the only occupant of the building. Under the same roof are Prime Meat Butcher and Deli and a thriving produce operation. The seafood market is in good company, as the three operations offer one-stop shopping for quality products to their many regular customers.

Superior Seafood owner Michael Elsas has been in the business for over twenty-five years and is an avid sports fisherman on the side. Prior to owning Superior, Elsas owned the Bonton Fish Market in Greenwich for nearly twenty years. At Superior, he is joined in the bright, shiny Westport market by his wife, Jessie, and their sons Jack and Jason, along with a small staff of skilled and dedicated workers.

Mike is an old hand at procuring the best seafood available in the region. He personally makes regular trips to the Fulton Fish Market at Hunts Point in the Bronx to select the best fish available from this major seafood distribution hub. Mike and his skilled staff then hand-cut all their boneless fillets in Superior's cutting room, ensuring top-notch product year-round. Certain whole fish for grilling or baking are available too.

There are two eye-popping seafood display cases front and center in the market, standing at right angles to each other. The right-hand case displays an amazing selection of freshly filleted and whole fish, such as swordfish steaks, sushi-grade tuna, halibut, fresh lemon sole, Scottish salmon, cod, mahimahi, snapper, brook trout fillets, and fresh whole branzino.

Turn the corner to the left for the shellfish and prepared foods display case. Here you'll find oysters, steamers, mussels, various varieties and sizes of raw shrimp, sea scallops, clams, cockles from New Zealand, and prepared seafoods such as fresh poached salmon salad, spicy chipotle crab spread, and homemade Maryland crab cakes. There's also a saltwater tank full of frisky hard-shell lobsters from Canada, which you may take home live or have steam-cooked by Superior's able staff.

All around the seafood counters is an ocean of fresh vegetables and other produce and several shelves of seafood complements and condiments. You won't need to go anywhere else to score your victuals for a complete, healthy meal. Add the adjacent butcher shop and deli into the mix, and you won't be left wanting, especially if you're shopping for a dinner party for family or friends.

The citizens of Westport are very fortunate to have this full-service seafood market in their midst, and it's worth a special trip if you're in the region and looking for quality seafood that's several cuts above what you'll find at the local supermarket. The Elsas family will make sure you leave their store with a smile on your face and some great seafood in your possession.

Seafood Marinara

Superior Seafood, Westport, Connecticut

3 garlic cloves, minced or cut in slices

¼ cup olive oil

½ onion, chopped

2 leeks, chopped

Salt

Pepper

Oregano

Red pepper flakes, to taste

½ cup white wine

2 jars marinara sauce

1 bottle clam juice

Fresh parsley

1 teaspoon Old Bay seasoning

18–24 clams

2 pounds mussels

1 pound shrimp

½ pound lobster meat

1 pound scallops

1 pound squid

This recipe makes a walloping amount of seafood marinara that can be served in bowls on its own or over fresh-cooked pasta. Freeze up the leftover sauce for later use—it only gets better over time.

In a large pot over medium heat on the stovetop, sauté the garlic in the olive oil until it's light brown. Add the onions, leeks, salt, pepper, oregano, and red pepper flakes. Add the wine and let it simmer until reduced by half, about 5 minutes.

Add the marinara sauce, clam juice, and parsley. Cover for a few minutes until it comes back to a light boil, then add the Old Bay seasoning, clams, mussels, shrimp, lobster, scallops, and squid, in that order. Cook until the clams and mussels have opened, approximately 15 minutes. Serves 6 to 8.

Tip: To simplify things, you can always use just one kind of seafood with this sauce, such as mussels or clams.

Seafood Combo Sauce

Champlin's Seafood, Narragansett, Rhode Island

4 ounces (1 stick) butter

1 teaspoon garlic powder

6 mussels

6 littleneck clams

½ pound 16/20-count raw shrimp, peeled and deveined

⅓ pound sea scallops (if large, cut in half)

⅓ pound chopped clams

1 ounce white wine

1 tablespoon lemon juice

½ jar red marinara sauce (optional)

This quick and simple seafood concoction from Champlin's in Rhode Island is best served over pasta or rice.

In a sauté pan over medium heat, melt the butter and sprinkle in the garlic powder. Add all the other ingredients, and cook until the mussels and clams open. Discard any that don't open. Serve over 1 pound of cooked pasta or 2 to 3 cups of cooked rice. Serves 4 to 5.

Linguine with White Clam Sauce

Bayley's Lobster Pound, Scarborough, Maine

1 pound linguine

¼ cup extra-virgin olive oil

1 teaspoon red pepper flakes
   (optional)

4 to 6 cloves garlic, finely chopped

2 tablespoons fresh thyme or
   1½ teaspoons dried

1 cup dry white wine

1 cup clam juice

1 pound clam meat, either
   chopped or whole and
   shucked

Juice of 1 lemon

¼ cup parsley leaves, chopped

Freshly ground black pepper and
   sea salt

This Italian-American classic packs a bit of heat in the form of crushed red pepper flakes. If you're not one for spicy food, you may leave them out, but the folks at Bayley's Lobster Pound, where the recipe originated, recommend that you leave them in.

Boil water in a large pot and cook the linguine until it is just *al dente*, then drain and set it aside.

While cooking the pasta, heat a large, deep skillet over medium heat. Add the olive oil, red pepper flakes, and garlic, and stir briefly. Add the thyme and wine, and reduce for 1 to 2 minutes. Add the clam juice. Stir in the clams and the juice of the lemon, and continue stirring until the mixture begins to steam.

Remove the skillet from the heat, and add the pasta to the skillet, mixing to blend. Add the parsley, and pepper and salt to taste. (You will want to have plenty of bread on hand to soak up the leftover sauce in the skillet.) Serves 4 to 6.

SEAFOOD CAKES

Atlantic Seafood Crab Cakes

Atlantic Seafood, Old Saybrook, Connecticut

½ pound crabmeat, fresh-picked

Salt to taste

Pepper to taste

1 teaspoon Old Bay Seasoning

1 teaspoon lemon juice

1 tablespoon onion, finely diced

1 tablespoon celery, finely diced

1 tablespoon mayonnaise

1 cup panko (or more, as necessary to bind the ingredients together)

¼ cup cooking oil

These crab cakes are made with tender loving care by Atlantic Seafood's chef Jerry Doran. Simplicity is the key, which makes them great candidates for cooking at home. The panko that the recipe calls for as a binder is a nice alternative taste and texture to the usual breadcrumbs.

Gently mix all ingredients except the cooking oil in a bowl, then set aside for 15 minutes. Form the mixture into four patties, each about 3 inches across and 1½ inches thick.

Heat the cooking oil in a heavy skillet over medium-high heat. Gently place the patties in the oil, and brown about 2 to 3 minutes per side. Remove from the pan and place the cakes on paper towels to drain for a minute or two. Serve with your favorite topping. Serves 4.

Citrus Salmon Cakes

Star Fish Market, Guilford, Connecticut

6 ounces wild pink salmon

½ cup crushed pretzels or crackers

½ cup (plus extra for drizzling)
   Earth & Vine Provisions–brand
   Key Lime Kiwi Tangerine
   Marinade and Dressing

2 tablespoons mayonnaise

1 clove garlic, crushed

Salt and pepper to taste

¼ cup all-purpose flour

3 tablespoons cooking oil

1 kiwi, peeled and sliced

Star Fish Market owner Mike Lukas says he receives constant requests for this recipe for salmon cakes—a staple that he prepares and keeps on hand daily in his store.

Mix together salmon, pretzels or crackers, ½ cup Key Lime Kiwi Tangerine Marinade, mayonnaise, and garlic. Form into 8 even-size patties. Mix the salt and pepper into the flour in a shallow dish. Heat the cooking oil in a medium-size skillet over medium heat. Coat the salmon cakes lightly on each side in the flour mixture. Place 4 salmon cakes at a time in the skillet and cook on each side until browned (about 2 minutes per side). Serve warm with extra Key Lime Kiwi Tangerine Marinade, and garnish with sliced kiwi. Serves 4.

Free Range Fish and Lobster

Portland, Maine

Free Range Fish and Lobster has experienced increasing amounts of success on the Portland waterfront over the past dozen years, since current owner Joe Ray bought the business out of bankruptcy in 2004. With the change in ownership, Free Range moved its fish-processing business down the street to a large facility next to Browne Trading Company, leaving the retail market in the original space at 450 Commercial Street, where it has flourished on its own for the past nine years.

With its black-and-gold motif and its whimsical red lobster sculpture protruding from the store's façade, Free Range literally stands out in a crowded market of seafood purveyors on the Portland waterfront. For starters, they're down toward the quieter end of Commercial Street, close to the Casco Bay Bridge. This makes parking in front of or close to the market significantly easier for customers than parking for similar waterfront locations closer to downtown.

General manager Cullen Burke presides over the market's day-to-day operations. He and his capable, knowledgeable staff wait on dozens and sometimes hundreds of customers each day. Keeping the twenty-plus linear feet of glassed-in seafood cases stocked can be a challenge. The fish is cut fresh in the back room, and a dedicated staff member picks upwards of 250 pounds of fresh lobster meat each day on gleaming, stainless steel tables in a separate processing room in back.

Inside the display cases are fresh fillets of flounder, haddock, pollock, cod, halibut, salmon, swordfish, tuna, and much more. Plump, tasty sea scallops, huge gulf shrimp, and calamari (squid) sit nearby. A broad array of fresh clams and oysters spill out of baskets over beds of ice on a table adjacent to the cases. Hanging suspended over the nearby lobster tank is a playful metal sculpture of a big, red lobster; a steel-wire rendition of a swordfish hangs from the wall over the oysters and clams.

In the middle of the market floor is a large table bearing fruits and vegetables and loaves of fresh-baked bread. Toward the front of the store are racks filled with spices, marinades, dressings, pastas, olive oil, breadcrumbs, panko, rice mixes, and a nice selection of wines. Everything you need for a fresh, healthy seafood dinner is right here. If you don't want to cook from scratch, try some of the prepared soups, chowders, appetizers, and meals in the refrigerated cases lining another wall.

Free Range Fish and Lobster is doing well in a crowded market, and you would do well to pay them a visit the next time you're in town!

Free Range Crab Cakes

Free Range Fish and Lobster, Portland, Maine

1 onion, diced

16 crackers, crushed (Free Range
    recommends Ritz crackers)

1 teaspoon mustard

1 teaspoon Worcestershire sauce

¼ cup mayonnaise

1 egg

1 pound crabmeat, cooked

2 tablespoons vegetable oil

BREADCRUMB COATING

½ cup unseasoned breadcrumbs

2 tablespoons dried parsley

2 tablespoons paprika

2 tablespoons Old Bay seasoning

In a large bowl, mix the onion thoroughly with the crushed crackers, mustard, Worcestershire, mayonnaise, and egg. Add the crabmeat and mix until all ingredients are combined throughout. Form into 4 to 5 individual cakes.

Mix the breadcrumb coating ingredients thoroughly in a separate bowl. Coat each crab patty with the breadcrumb mixture.

Pan fry the cakes in a lightly oiled pan on medium heat for about 3–4 minutes on each side, or until the egg is cooked. Serves 4 for appetizer, 2 for main course.

Shackford and Gooch Salt Codfish Cakes

Clam Shack Seafood Market, Kennebunk, Maine

1 pound salt cod

2 pounds Maine potatoes, cut into 1-inch chunks

4 tablespoons butter

½ teaspoon ground black pepper

⅓–½ cup light cream

Bacon grease, butter, or olive oil for frying

Shackford and Gooch Fish Market—Clam Shack Seafood's predecessor—packed and sold their own salt cod, a version of the famous fish that has been heavily salted, dried, and preserved. Back in the day, fishermen delivered their catch of cod directly from their boats to the seafood market's back door, right on the Kennebunk River wharf. Shackford and Gooch used to market and sell their salt codfish under the Port Brand Cod name. It was one of the nation's most popular salt cod brands in the 1940s and 1950s. Take a walk down memory lane, and give this recipe a try.

Soak the salt cod overnight in cold water, changing the water twice and keeping the cod refrigerated throughout. Drain off the water, place the cod in a saucepan with water to cover, and simmer until the fish flakes, about 15 to 20 minutes.

Meanwhile, boil the potatoes in salted water until they're tender. Drain the water, return the potatoes to the pot, and mash. Drain the fish and let it cool. Pick out any bones or skin.

Add the fish, butter, and pepper to the potatoes, and beat, using a wooden spoon. Add cream to make a smooth but stiff batter. Shape the batter into six ½-inch-thick patties, and fry gently in bacon grease, butter, or olive oil for 3 to 4 minutes per side, or until golden. Serves 6.

Maine Crab Cakes

Trenton Bridge Lobster Pound, Trenton, Maine

1 cup Italian seasoned
   breadcrumbs

1 large or 2 small eggs

¼ cup mayonnaise

½ teaspoon salt

¼ teaspoon pepper

1 teaspoon Worcestershire sauce

1 teaspoon dry mustard

1 pound crabmeat

2 tablespoons cooking oil

These crab cakes are particularly good when they're made with fresh meat from rock crabs (also known as "peekytoe" crabs) or Jonah crabs, both natives of Maine waters. Both types are generally available in seafood markets throughout New England seasonally.

Mix the crumbs, eggs, mayonnaise, and seasonings. Fold in the crabmeat. Mix gently and thoroughly, then shape into 5 or 6 patties. Warm the cooking oil in a pan, then fry the crab cakes about 5 minutes on each side until they are light brown. Serves 5 to 6 as an appetizer, or 3 as a main course.

Pinkham's Seafood

Boothbay, Maine

Located about three miles up the road from Boothbay Harbor and roughly equidistant between the tidal Sheepscot and Damariscotta rivers, Pinkham's Seafood is ideally situated to serve Boothbay Harbor's residents and tourists and to harvest fresh shellfish (especially clams) from the nearby rivers. Known as the go-to place for clams in mid-coast Maine, the seafood market has thrived in this spot for over thirty years.

Larry and Susan Pinkham established Pinkham's in the early 1980s, when it initially served as a clam-shucking operation for local wholesalers in addition to being a seafood market. The Pinkhams' son Russell began his career as a commercial fisherman around the same time. In 2008, Susan Pinkham fell ill, and Russell stepped up to help out with the business, which he bought from his parents the following year. Pinkham's is now owned by Russell and his wife, Cathy, and is housed in a bright, cheery, cedar-shingled building in plain sight along the east side of Route 27.

Inside the market is a glass case filled with the catches of the day, which can be anything from haddock, cod, salmon, swordfish, tuna, and halibut to the famed local clams, steamers, periwinkles (sea snails), scallops, crabmeat, and lobsters. Cathy also cooks up a variety of chowders and stews that are available to eat on the spot or for carryout.

This simple roadside stand is the ideal place to pick up some fresh seafood or a snack when going to or coming from the Boothbay Harbor area. And if you're a big fan of steamed clams in particular, you're in for a real treat.

Clam Cakes

Pinkham's Seafood, Boothbay, Maine

1 quart chopped clams in juice

1 medium onion, chopped fine

2 large eggs

3½ sleeves Ritz crackers, crushed

½ teaspoon salt

½ teaspoon pepper

Flour

Butter or Crisco oil for frying

Clam cakes, also referred to as clam fritters, are typically hush puppy–like balls of fried dough or cake flecked with clam bits. At Pinkham's Seafood in Boothbay, Maine, they prefer to make them into flat patties, which are actually easier to fry up in a pan at home.

In a large bowl, mix the clams, onion, eggs, crackers, salt, and pepper. The mixture will be fairly wet but can be easily molded into firm patties about ¼ inch thick. Roll the patties in flour, and fry them in the oil or butter in the pan over medium heat. Brown on each side. Remove the patties and allow them to drain on paper towels. Serve with tarter sauce or with your favorite chowder. Makes 10 to 12 clam cakes.

McLaughlin's Crab Cakes

McLaughlin's Seafood, Bangor, Maine

1 pound fresh Maine crabmeat

¼ cup onions, diced

¼ cup celery, diced

1 egg

1 tablespoon Old Bay seasoning

1 tablespoon Worcestershire sauce

½ tablespoon spicy brown mustard

½ teaspoon black pepper

¾ cup mayonnaise

¼ cup crushed Ritz crackers

¼ cup cooking oil

McLaughlin's serves these at their fish market seafood stand and at their riverside restaurant, Mclaughlin's at the Marina. The crushed Ritz crackers are a nice alternative to breadcrumbs and other fillers.

Squeeze the juice out of the crabmeat and place the dry crabmeat into a large mixing bowl. Dice up the onions and celery and add them to the crabmeat. Add all the other ingredients to the bowl and mix thoroughly, except the cooking oil.

Try making a patty with your hands; if it holds together well, then you are all set to continue; if not, then add ¼ cup more mayonnaise to help the patties stick together better. Make all the patties the same size.

Heat the cooking oil in a skillet over medium heat. Place the patties in the heated oil. Brown the patties on each side, checking to make sure they have been heated through, and serve. Makes six 3-ounce crab cakes.

Wulf's Fish Cakes

Wulf's Fish Market, Brookline, Massachusetts

2 russet potatoes, cooked and crumbled into soft chunks

1 pound grey sole

1 pound haddock

2 onions, chopped

2 eggs, beaten

Salt

Pepper

3 tablespoons cooking oil

Breadcrumbs

Longtime Wulf's Fish Market manager Richie Taylor is partial to this simple recipe for fish cakes, which can be whipped together and served in a snap. These cakes are particularly good in the wintertime with a chowder or bisque.

Peel and boil the potatoes for 10 to 15 minutes, then set them aside to cool.

Finely chop the sole and haddock. Mix in the chopped onions, crumbled potatoes, and eggs. Salt and pepper to taste. Shape the mixture by hand into 6 to 7 patties.

Heat the cooking oil over medium-high heat in a large skillet. Roll the patties in breadcrumbs and fry them until they're golden brown. Serves 5 to 6.

Chatham Pier Crab Cakes

Chatham Pier Fish Market, Chatham, Massachusetts

6 pounds crabmeat

1 tablespoon fresh lemon juice

½ teaspoon Tabasco sauce

2 tablespoons Worcestershire sauce

2 tablespoons Grey Poupon Dijon mustard

1 cup diced onion

½ cup diced celery

¼ cup diced red bell pepper

¼ cup diced green bell pepper

1 teaspoon diced fresh garlic

¼ cup dry parsley flakes

3 cups panko or breadcrumbs

EGG WASH

6 eggs

1½ cups water

3 cups dried panko

4 tablespoons (½ stick) salted butter

These crab cakes from Chatham Pier are a bit more exotic than most, with an egg wash, Dijon mustard, diced bell pepper, and parsley flakes. And they're chock full of tasty crabmeat, the key ingredient for any good crab cake recipe.

Mix all of the ingredients, except the eggs, water, panko, and butter in a large mixing bowl, adding the crabmeat last, to make sure the crabmeat stays intact. Using your clean hands, form the mixture into 15 flat, round cakes about 3 inches in diameter and ¾ inch thick. Set aside.

Make an egg wash by combining the eggs and water in a shallow dish, and whisking thoroughly. Dip the formed cakes gently into the egg wash, then coat each one on all sides with panko or breadcrumbs. Let the cakes stand and firm up in the refrigerator for at least 2 hours.

Melt the butter in a large skillet, and sauté the cakes in batches on both sides until a golden amber color is achieved, about 3 minutes per side. Serve warm. Makes 15 cakes.

GRILLED FISH

City Fish Market

Wethersfield, Connecticut

This multigenerational, Greek-American family-owned seafood dynasty rules the roost in the retail and wholesale seafood world of central Connecticut. A major wholesaler in Connecticut and Rhode Island, City Fish's distinctive yellow trucks with black lettering and golden fish hook on the sides may be seen throughout southern New England year-round, making deliveries to restaurants and quality food retailers with a need for consistently good, fresh seafood products.

City Fish has its own excellent retail seafood market on Silas Deane Highway in Wethersfield, several miles south of Hartford. It's one of those rare and exciting shops where the retail portion sits in the midst of a large, warehouse-like space, where fish deliveries and orders are processed and trans-

ported to and fro, wheeled on dollies across concrete floors regularly sprayed down with water to keep things fresh, cool, and clean.

A bit of history: Genos Anagnos started City Fish on Main Street in Hartford in 1930, no doubt a tough time to start a business. After relocating to Front Street in Hartford, the company made the move to its current home in Wethersfield in 1967, which is the same year City Fish opened its retail market.

And what a retail market it is! The massive, glass-encased seafood counter is stuffed chockablock daily with all sorts of wonderfully fresh seafood from City Fish's 70,000-cubic-foot cold-storage room. (There's also a 100,000-cubic-foot deep freezer used mostly for the wholesale business.) You probably won't find cheaper, better swordfish steaks in the area, with specials on the hand-cut fillets featured regularly. There's also a 5,000-gallon lobster pound that regularly stocks red guys weighing anywhere from one to ten pounds.

Current CEO John Anagnos (Genos's grandson) has seven children, four of whom are in the business. Daughter Davina has become the heart and soul of City Fish, holding various management positions over the years while keeping a steady stream of wonderful recipes posted on their website and sent out to their extensive email list of customers. Davina's brother Telly runs the retail operation, brother George is City Fish's main buyer, and sister Michele handles most of the market's business and administrative tasks.

Around the corner from the seafood counter is a dine-in-the-rough, fresh-cooked seafood stand with excellent fish and chips and regionally famous lobster rolls, served both warm with butter or chilled with mayo. There's even an air-conditioned dining room tricked out with tables, televisions, beer on tap, and wine by the glass just behind the retail seafood counter. Customers have held parties, even wedding rehearsal dinners there, as it accommodates nearly a hundred people. With all the different goings-on at City Fish, it begins to take on the atmosphere of a seafood theme park of sorts.

As one might imagine, City Fish's clout in the New England seafood market allows it to get top-quality fish and shellfish from its suppliers on a regular basis. The company runs its own semi-tractor-trailer truck to and from the main seafood market in Boston three times a week. In addition, numerous other regional, national, even international suppliers do a lot of business with City Fish. This benefits the retail market through plentiful supplies and extended seasons for often hard-to-get items.

Take a trip on the Silas Deane Highway, and keep your eyes peeled for the distinctive yellow and white awnings on the City Fish building. Plan on stocking up on plenty of fresh seafood and prepared foods of all sorts—and plan on staying for lunch!

Telly Anagnos of City Fish Market

Lemon Pepper Grilled Halibut

City Fish Market, Wethersfield, Connecticut

¼ cup fresh lemon juice

1 large garlic clove, pressed

1 10- to 12-ounce halibut fillet
    (about 1½ inches thick)

Olive oil

1 teaspoon lemon peel, minced

Pepper and salt

Lemon wedges

Halibut is a large, meaty fish that performs very well on the grill. Here's a Mediterranean version of sorts from the Greek-American–owned City Fish Market in Wethersfield, Connecticut.

Place the lemon juice and garlic clove in a baking dish, and allow the garlic to infuse the lemon juice (about 10 to 15 minutes). Add the halibut and turn to coat. Refrigerate for 30 minutes to 1 hour.

Preheat the grill to medium-high heat, making sure the cooking grates are clean. Brush the halibut with olive oil, then rub the fillet with the minced lemon peel. Season generously with pepper, then with salt to taste.

Grill the halibut until cooked through, turning once, about 8 minutes total. The fillet should begin to flake at the touch of a fork. Remove from the grill, divide into serving-size portions, transfer to serving plates, and serve with lemon wedges. Serves 2.

Grilled Block Island Swordfish with Grilled Corn on the Cob

Bud's Fish Market, Branford, Connecticut

2 swordfish steaks, 1–1¼ pounds
each

Bottled fish marinade (any kind
will work)

4–6 ears fresh corn on the cob

1 lemon

Salt and pepper, to taste

Butter

Swordfish is one of the easiest, most forgiving types of fish fillets to grill, as it's firm and holds together well while being cooked and turned. Although the name of this recipe, from Bud's Market in Branford, Connecticut, calls for Block Island swordfish, you can use any swordfish you find in your local market.

Marinate the swordfish steaks in the refrigerator for 1 hour before cooking, using the fish marinade.

Remove some husks from the corn, pull back to remove the silk, and re-cover with the remaining husks. Submerge the ears in a bucket of water for 15 minutes. Drain the ears, and grill for 10 to 15 minutes over medium heat, turning every few minutes with tongs to allow the corn to cook uniformly. Remove the cooked ears from the grill, and set aside.

Turn the grill up to medium high heat. Grill the swordfish for 8 minutes per side, until the middle of the fish flakes a bit at the touch of a fork.

Serve the fillets with lemon slices and the corn with salt, pepper, and butter. Serves 4 to 6.

Grilled Grouper with Lemon/Herb Sauce

City Fish Market, Wethersfield, Connecticut

2-pound grouper fillet, cut into 4 serving pieces

2–4 tablespoons extra virgin olive oil

2 teaspoons sea salt

4 tablespoons butter

3 tablespoons fresh parsley or basil, chopped fine

½ cup lemon juice

½ cup half & half

Sea salt and cracked black pepper to taste

Although grouper is a fish more commonly associated with Florida and other waters in the south, and with South America, a number of fish markets in New England regularly stock it, as it's a very versatile and popular fish for grilling and frying. Here's a nice recipe for grilling grouper in a Mediterranean style.

Coat the fish with olive oil and season with sea salt on both sides. Place the fish on a preheated, hot grill and cook until the edges of the fish pieces turn white, approximately 5 minutes, then turn and cook an additional 5 minutes or until the fish easily flakes with a fork.

In a small saucepan on the stove or a side burner of the grill, combine the butter and herbs. When the butter is melted, add the lemon juice and half & half, then whisk. Bring to a boil. Remove the lemon/herb sauce from the heat, plate the fish, and pour the sauce over the fish. Serves 4.

Bud's Maple Grilled Plank Salmon

Bud's Fish Market, Branford, Connecticut

1 cedar cooking plank (18 inches long, 6 inches wide, ½ inch thick)

1 large (1–2 pounds) fillet of salmon (skin on)

4 tablespoons pure maple syrup (brown sugar is an acceptable substitute)

Pepper to taste

2–3 teaspoons dill weed, fresh chopped (optional)

Cooking fish fillets on the grill using wooden planks as a buffer between the flames and the fish is an excellent way to prepare seafood, particularly large fish fillets. The wood adds a nice, smoky flavor to the fish, and it also protects the fillets from sticking to the metal grates of the grill. Lots of seafood stores sell small planks of various types of wood: hickory, cherry, cedar, oak, maple, and more. Give it a try!

Soak the cooking plank in water for about 1 hour. Marinate the fish in the maple syrup for 30 minutes to 1 hour; sprinkle the pepper over the meat side of the salmon fillet; then sprinkle on the dill weed.

Place the salmon, skin side down, on the grilling plank. Cover the grill and cook for 12 to 15 minutes per pound or until the salmon flakes when pierced with a fork. Do not turn over. The smoke emanating from the slowly charring wood plank will yield a lot of smoky flavor. Serves 4.

Tuna Steaks with Hoisin Ginger Marinade

R&D Seafood, Woonsocket, Rhode Island

2 teaspoons sesame oil

2 tablespoons soy sauce

3 tablespoons sherry wine

2 tablespoons hoisin sauce

Salt and pepper, to taste

1 teaspoon garlic, chopped

1 teaspoon ginger, finely chopped

4 6-ounce tuna steaks

Tuna steaks are a bit trickier to grill than swordfish, but this tasty marinated version gives you lots of flavor and a bigger window of cooking time, minimizing the chance of drying out the fish while it's cooking.

Combine the sesame oil, soy sauce, sherry, hoisin sauce, salt, pepper, garlic and ginger in a flat baking dish. Coat the fresh tuna steaks in the marinade, and refrigerate for up to one hour in the baking dish, turning occasionally for even coverage.

Preheat the grill to medium-high heat. Grill the tuna steaks 3 to 4 minutes per side, or until the fish begins to flake when tested with a fork but is still pink in the center. Remove the fish from the grill and let it stand for several minutes to allow the cooking process to finish. Serve with steamed rice pilaf and a fresh tossed salad on the side. Serves 4.

Presidential Swordfish

Clam Shack Seafood Market, Kennebunk, Maine

MARINADE

1 teaspoon coarse salt

1 teaspoon coarse ground pepper

½ teaspoon dried onion

½ teaspoon dried garlic

½ teaspoon crushed red pepper

½ teaspoon dried thyme

½ teaspoon dried rosemary

¼ teaspoon dried coriander

2 cups mayonnaise

⅓ cup lemon juice

4 swordfish steaks, 6–8 ounces
each

Clam Shack Seafood Market keeps presidential swordfish stocked and ready for whenever President George H. W. Bush calls. Beloved neighbors and loyal customers, Clam Shack Seafood has a decades-long relationship with the Bush family and their Walker's Point staff. This recipe was handed down by longtime Bush family chef Ariel Guzman, who adapted it from a family friend's recipe. Clam Shack Seafood has doctored it a bit to make their own version.

In a small bowl, whisk together all the dry ingredients. In a larger bowl, whisk together the mayonnaise and lemon juice. Add the dry ingredients to the mayonnaise and lemon juice, and stir until smooth.

Place the swordfish steaks in a large, sealable plastic bag. Pour in the marinade, and move around the contents of the bag to make sure it covers and coats the steaks thoroughly. Refrigerate in the bag on a plate for at least 3 hours.

Preheat the outdoor grill. Grill the swordfish steaks over high heat for about 2 minutes per side, anticipating flare-ups from the marinade. The steaks will be ivory in color and golden brown around the edges when done. Serves 4.

Grilled Salmon with Salsa Verde

City Fish Market, Wethersfield, Connecticut

2 pounds salmon fillets

1 cup Italian salad dressing
(bottled is fine)

SALSA VERDE

1 cup fresh parsley, chopped

½ cup olive oil

¼ cup scallions, chopped (green
tops only)

¼ cup capers, drained

1 lemon, juiced

1 tablespoon garlic, minced

1 teaspoon fresh thyme, chopped

1 teaspoon fresh oregano, chopped

½ teaspoon fresh rosemary,
chopped

½ teaspoon fresh sage, chopped

Salt and pepper to taste

This recipe for grilling salmon calls for a relatively simple marinating and grilling method, combined with a heady salsa verde served over the top or on the side.

Preheat the grill to a high temperature, making sure the grates are free of char before the grilling begins. Marinate the salmon in the salad dressing for 15 minutes.

Grill the fillets over high heat for 4 to 5 minutes per side. The fish is cooked when the flesh is translucent and flaky to the touch of a fork. Divide the fillets into serving portions and move to a serving platter. Serves 6.

For the salsa verde, mix all the ingredients in large bowl. Season with salt and pepper to taste. Let stand for at least 30 minutes to allow the flavors to come together. Serve over or alongside the grilled salmon.

Lemon-Soy Grilled Swordfish

Nauset Fish and Lobster Pool, Orleans, Massachusetts

MARINADE

4 garlic cloves, minced

⅓ cup white wine

¼ cup lemon juice

2 tablespoons soy sauce

2 tablespoons olive oil

1 tablespoon poultry seasoning

Salt and pepper to taste

1 pound swordfish fillets

Lemon slices and parsley for
    garnish

This swordfish marinade is easy to make and brings out new dimensions from this flavorful fish.

Place all the ingredients except the fillets, lemon slices, and parsley in a shallow baking dish and mix well. Place the fillets in the mix, flipping them over once or twice for a thorough coating, then refrigerate for 1 hour. Grill the fillets over high heat for 5 to 6 minutes per side. Remove from the grill and let stand for a few minutes to let the cooking finish. Garnish with lemon slices on the side and parsley sprigs on the top. Serves 2.

Whole Striped Bass with Fresh Herbs

Clam Shack Seafood Market, Kennebunk, Maine

1 striped bass, 2+ pounds, cleaned and scaled

1 tablespoon butter, softened

1 teaspoon coarse salt

½ teaspoon coarse ground pepper

1 lemon, sliced thin

6–8 sprigs fresh herbs (mint, rosemary, parsley, thyme or bay—use a combination that appeals to you or whatever's fresh in the garden.)

Olive oil

Clam Shack Seafood is located right on the tidal Kennebunk River. Seagulls and mallard ducks sit under the porch rails, waiting for customers to drop snacks into the water. The birds have extra competition with the striped bass that come in on the high tide and know a good feeding spot when they find one.

The seafood market has a live "Striper Cam" installed on a piling underwater, and customers in the market watching a television screen have a real fish-eye view of the stripers as they swim past the lens. Though it's not legal to sell striped bass in Maine, recreational fishermen and charter boats are allowed to fish for and keep their stripers, if they're of legal size. When one of the local charter fishing guides shares his catch with seafood market owner Steve Kingston, here's how he likes to prepare it for his family and friends at home.

Preheat the outdoor grill. Clean and dry the cavity of the fish. Rub the inside with butter, salt, and pepper. Line the inside with a few lemon slices, and fill the cavity with whole, loosely packed herbs.

Close up the striper with skewers or twine. Rub the outside with olive oil and salt and pepper.

Grill 8 minutes on the first side, then carefully turn and cook the striper for 6 to 7 minutes on the other. Serves 3 to 4, depending on the size of the fish.

Grilled Teriyaki Swordsteaks

Kyler's Catch Seafood Market, New Bedford, Massachusetts

1 pound swordfish steak

1 tablespoon olive oil

¼ cup teriyaki sauce

1 teaspoon Dijon mustard

½ teaspoon minced garlic

2 tablespoons capers, crushed

Capers give this quick, simple recipe for grilled swordfish a pleasantly distinctive flavor.

Preheat the grill to high. Grill the swordfish for 5 to 7 minutes per side, until it's flaky to the touch of a fork. Set it aside to allow the cooking to finish.

At the same time, combine the remaining ingredients in a small sauté pan and simmer for 3 minutes. Pour the resulting sauce over the grilled swordfish. Serves 2 to 3.

Whole Grilled Dorade

Wulf's Fish Market, Brookline, Massachusetts

8 garlic cloves, chopped

12 thyme sprigs

Olive oil

2 lemons

2 whole dorade, approximately 2 pounds each, clipped, scaled, and gutted with the head on (you may want to have your local fish market do this)

Kosher salt

Fresh cracked pepper

The dorade, also known as sea bream, is a fish from the Mediterranean Sea. It's highly valued in Europe for its firm flesh and its wonderful flavor. Wulf's Fish Market in Brookline, Massachusetts, regularly stocks whole dorade, and this is their recommended recipe for cooking it up in the oven (though it's great on the grill, also).

Preheat the oven to 450 degrees and the grill to high.

In a bowl, mix the chopped garlic, thyme, olive oil, and the juice of one lemon together. Score the fish on both sides, and season generously with salt and pepper. Cover each dorade with the garlic/thyme mixture. (Make sure to get the inside cavity of the fish, also.) Quarter the remaining lemon, and put the lemon slices inside the fish bellies. Let the fish marinate for 20 minutes.

Place the fish on a roasting rack above a sheet tray, and cook for approximately 20 to 25 minutes. Then transfer to fish to the grill and cook for approximately 6 minutes per side, until the flesh on the inside is flaky. Let the dorade rest for 5 minutes before serving. Serves 4.

LOBSTER

Bayley's Lobster Pound

Scarborough, Maine

Few seafood markets anywhere have the roots and the traditions that Bayley's Lobster Pound of Pine Point (Scarborough), Maine, can boast. The lobster pound and seafood market celebrated its 100th year of operations in 2015.

Today's business looks nothing like the one that Stephen and Ella Bayley started as a young couple, when they moved from Wells, Maine, to Pine Point in 1915. In addition to working at the nearby Snow clam-processing plant, Stephen dug clams in the rich beds of Jones Creek and trapped lobsters offshore to help feed his family. When there were leftover lobsters, Ella would cook them up in her kitchen and sell them through the kitchen window to neighbors and passersby.

Stephen grew his lobster fishing into a wholesale business of its own and bought a small shack in Pine Point to serve as his base of operations. When he and his partner had excess inventory at the end of the day, they would occasionally pack live lobsters and seaweed into a few suitcases, hop the local passenger train, and ride up to nearby Portland to sell the lobsters there.

The Bayley family no longer has to ride the rails, as their business has grown into a thriving retail market, which opened in the 1950s, an ongoing lobster wholesale business, and a recently christened restaurant and bar that sits on a lovely wooden pier extending over the adjacent Nonesuch River, with its serene wetlands and bird life.

Before we get to the seafood market proper, let's pause at the outdoor lobster tanks next to the market's front door. At any given time, and especially in the heat of summer, these holding tanks are bursting with fresh, live lobsters recently caught and delivered by more than a dozen local lobster fishermen. You may pick your own hardshell or softshell "bug" from the many crawling around the coldwater tanks, then take it home live or have Bayley's cook it up in their massive boilers on the premises. These cookers emit a wonderfully aromatic steam that gives the entire place the scent of fresh-cooked lobster and briny seawater.

Inside the market itself are a couple of long glass cases stocked with super-fresh fish fillets and shellfish in an amazing variety. Peer through the frosted glass to behold swordfish steaks, fresh haddock and halibut fillets, locally sourced sea scallops and clams, and raw and cooked shrimp, among other delicacies. There are fresh salmon fillets as well as tasty chunks of smoked salmon, which Bayley's makes in its own smoker.

Be sure to try one of Bayley's homemade cold lobster rolls. They claim to have invented the Maine lobster roll back in the 1920s, and there's no reason to doubt them. (Their simple recipe for a "Maine's Original Lobster Roll" appears on page 127.)

If you're in the market for some fresh-picked lobster meat, this is one of the best seafood markets for it. Veteran lobster picker Jodi Libby de-shells hundreds of lobsters on a busy day, and much of that succulent lobster meat goes into airtight plastic containers, which you'll find in the display cases. Bayley's does all the tough work of picking the meat, so you can focus on making your lobster rolls, lobster salad, lobster stew, or whatever you fancy.

With 100 years of family experience in the lobster and seafood businesses, Bayley's Lobster Pound is tough to beat for quality and consistency. Pay their market a visit when you're in southern Maine, then have a lobster roll and a beer on the dock before returning home with your "catch."

Maine Lobster Pie

Bayley's Lobster Pound, Scarborough, Maine

8 tablespoons (1 stick) butter

1 pound lobster meat, fresh-picked
    and cut into bite-size pieces

2 cups leeks, chopped

5 tablespoons flour

2½ cups heavy cream

3 egg yolks

¼ cup sherry

1 puff pastry sheet, thawed

1 egg, beaten

Lobster pie is a staple of coastal Maine, and this super-rich version from Bayley's Lobster Pound, a nationally renowned purveyor of fresh lobster, is guaranteed to please lobster lovers of all stripes.

Preheat the oven to 400 degrees. Melt the butter in a saucepan over medium heat and sauté the lobster meat in it until you see a bit of red coloring. Remove the lobster meat and portion it evenly into four small baking dishes.

Add the chopped leeks to the butter and sauté until it's soft. Add the flour and stir to make a roux-like paste. Slowly add in the heavy cream, and heat until the mixture is thick and bubbly. Add 3 tablespoons of the cream sauce to the egg yolks and combine, and then pour the egg yolk mixture back into the cream sauce. Add the sherry to the sauce, and whisk to combine.

Pour the cream mixture over the lobster in each baking dish, and cover each with the puff pastry sheet, cutting the pastry sheet to fit over the tops of the baking dishes. Brush the top of each puff pastry sheet with beaten egg and bake for 12 minutes, or until each pastry sheet is puffed up and brown. Serves 4.

Three Ways to Cook a Lobster

Here are three different methods for cooking lobster from three of the top purveyors of lobster in the state of Maine. Choose the one that looks and feels best for you. Whichever one you choose, you really can't go wrong.

How to Cook a Perfect Maine Lobster

(from the Clam Shack Seafood Market; Kennebunkport, Maine)

To us, a 1¼-pound Maine lobster is the perfect size. At that size, they're sweet and tender, big enough to satisfy, but still small enough that you can eat two. Cooking it correctly is imperative. We recommend cooking your lobster in a large, uncrowded pot of rapidly boiling salt water. If the ocean isn't at your doorstep, just go three times around your pot with high-quality coarse salt.

When the water is boiling, toss your lobsters in and cover the pot tightly. Keep them at a boil for 15 minutes, or until they float.

Get the butter and lemon ready!

Steamed Lobster

(from Jess's Market; Rockland, Maine)

Put about 1 inch of water and a handful of salt in a pot, and then bring the water to a rapid boil. Once the water is boiling, put the lobsters in and cover the pot. Once steam starts coming out around edges of the cover, start your timer, using the guidelines below.

Hardshell Lobsters: 1¼ pounds—cook 20 minutes. 1½ pounds—cook 20–25 minutes. 3–4 pounds—cook 40–45 minutes.

Softshell Lobsters: 1¼ pounds—cook 15 minutes. 1½ pounds— cook 20 minutes.

Lobsters may be re-heated in the microwave or by steaming again for a short period.

Tip: If you order lobsters via overnight shipment, they should be removed from the box, put in a paper bag, and refrigerated as soon as they arrive. Do not put your lobsters in standing water. Cook them as soon as possible—do not wait until they die. They will usually survive in your refrigerator for several days, but they should always be cooked at any sign of weakness. They can always be re-heated, once cooked, or picked and eaten chilled.

Simple Boiled Lobster

(from Bayley's Lobster Pound; Scarborough, Maine)

1 ounce sea salt
1 quart water
1 medium (1¼ pound) live Maine lobster

Bring the water to a boil. Drop the lobster into the pot head-first (if you put it in tail-first, you risk being splashed with boiling water). Cover the pot. Start timing from the moment that you put the lobster into the pot. A medium hard-shell lobster will take about 20 minutes, and a medium soft-shell only about 15 minutes.

It is important to note that it is very difficult to overcook lobsters. When they are cooked longer, they become more tender. However, when you undercook a lobster, you run the risk of not having the tomalley (liver) of the lobster fully cooked. The tomalley turns green only when fully cooked. If it is not fully cooked, it will be a blackish, oily substance when you open up the lobster. This is why we always suggest erring on the side of adding a few extra minutes if you are not sure. It is fine to cook several lobsters at the same time as long as the water is able to come back to a boil during the cooking process.

Lobster Salad

Atlantic Seafood, Old Saybrook, Connecticut

8 ounces lobster meat, cooked, fresh-picked, and coarsely chopped

1 tablespoon sweet Vidalia onion, finely diced

1 tablespoon celery, finely diced

Dashes of salt and black pepper

Juice of ½ lemon

Dash of hot sauce

Pinch of Old Bay seasoning

Just enough mayonnaise to coat lobster

This tried-and-true recipe for cold lobster salad is great on a top-split, buttered, toasted hot dog bun in the form of a cold lobster roll. It can also be served over a bed of greens as an excellent lobster-laced salad.

Combine all ingredients in a bowl and mix thoroughly. Set aside and cool in the refrigerator for 1 hour to let the flavors come together. Serve in split-top hot dog buns or over a bed of greens. Serves 2.

Lobster Quiche

Port Lobster Company, Kennebunkport, Maine

1 pint heavy whipping cream

4 eggs

2 tablespoons sherry

8 ounces fresh-picked lobster meat
(crabmeat may be substituted)

1 cup Swiss cheese, shredded

1 frozen pie shell (slightly thawed)

This seafood quiche recipe is guaranteed to please any time of day or year. It's quick and simple and serves up nicely for breakfast, lunch, or dinner.

Preheat the oven to 425 degrees. In a medium bowl with a wire whisk, mix the cream, eggs, and sherry until well blended.

Place the lobster or crabmeat and the shredded cheese into the pie shell. Pour the cream mixture over the lobster meat or crabmeat and cheese. Bake for 15 minutes. Turn the oven temperature down to 325 degrees, and continue baking for 35 minutes or until a knife or toothpick inserted in the center comes out clean. Serves 4.

Mac's Seafood-Stuffed Lobster

Mac's Seafood, Wellfleet, Massachusetts

LOBSTER

1 3-pound lobster (or two
    1½-pound lobsters)

¼ cup sea salt

SEAFOOD STUFFING

½ cup red pepper, finely diced

½ cup red onion, finely diced

¼ pound large or extra-large
    shrimp, shells and tails
    removed

¼ pound sea scallops

2–3 cups panko (Japanese
    breadcrumbs)

1 cup parsley, roughly chopped

½ teaspoon baking powder

½ lemon, freshly squeezed

½ cup (1 stick) melted butter,
    divided

1 tablespoon mayonnaise
    (optional)

4 or 5 dashes Tabasco or Sriracha

½ teaspoon Old Bay seasoning

½ teaspoon salt

¼ teaspoon pepper

Salted butter, melted (to serve with
    the finished dish)

Lemon wedges

Here is a very elaborate and wonderfully sophisticated way to make stuffed lobster. This recipe comes from one of the premier seafood purveyors on Cape Cod, and it is well worth all the effort needed to make it.

Par-cook the lobster in boiling salted water for 3 minutes. Remove and cool in an ice bath.

Remove the claws, and split the lobster down the middle with a sharp knife. Remove the tomalley (the green matter, which is the lobster's liver), and reserve the lobster roe. (See Tip for optional lobster roe preparation.) Wash out the body cavity. Remove the claw and knuckle meat, keeping the claw meat intact, if possible. Set aside the knuckle meat to add to the seafood stuffing.

Sweat the red pepper and red onion in a bit of melted butter. Sweating is a technique used to draw out moisture and soften aromatic vegetables like onions or peppers without browning them. The key is to cook the vegetables on a low heat until they are soft—or in the case of onions, translucent. This will enhance their essence and build a flavor base for the seafood stuffing.

Cut the shrimp and scallops into bite-size pieces, and add to the pan. Sauté for 2 to 3 minutes or until cooked about halfway through. Slightly toast the panko in a dry, nonstick pan over medium heat. Melt the rest of the butter, and fold the rest of the seafood stuffing ingredients into a mixing bowl.

Preheat the oven to 375 degrees. Fill the lobster body cavity with the seafood stuffing. Fluff the seafood stuffing with a fork, using a light touch when adding to the body cavity. If you overstuff or pack down the stuffing, it will not cook prop-

erly. Press the lobster claw meat into the stuffing and bake for 10 to 12 minutes. Finish under a broiler for 2 minutes or until the seafood stuffing is golden brown. Serve with melted butter and a lemon wedge. Serves 2 to 3.

Tip: Lobster roe, also known as "coral," is the eggs found in the body cavity of a female lobster. The eggs are naturally black and turn a beautiful bright coral red when cooked. To prepare the lobster roe, gently whisk to break up the eggs, and add them to a pan of hot melted butter on the stove for about 1 minute or until the eggs turn red. Fold the buttery roe into the seafood stuffing mixture, if desired.

David's Fish Market and Lobster Pound

Salisbury, Massachusetts

Housed in a stark-white, cinder block building on U.S. 1 in the border town of Salisbury, Massachusetts, David's Fish Market is in an enviable position, sitting as it does near the three oceanside magnets of Newburyport and Salisbury, Massachusetts, and Seabrook, New Hampshire. It's also near the mouth of the Merrimack River. During the summer months, this area is swamped with tourists, beachgoers, and seaside cottage dwellers, all of them relying on David's for a steady supply of excellent seafood. (As if that's not enough, David's also sits near the confluence of I-95 and I-495, making it a convenient place to shop when traveling between Boston and Maine.)

David's got its start shortly after World War II, in 1946, when Arthur "A.J." David, who had been delivering and selling fish to his customers by bicycle, opened a retail store on Route 1 in Salisbury. He built the business over the next few decades, then sold it to his great grandson Gordon Blaney in 1972. Gordon, who has been involved with the business for over fifty years, continues to own and run David's Fish to this day, and several other family members are active in the business.

David's is the go-to place for fresh lobster in the Massachusetts–New Hampshire border area. They keep their aquamarine lobster tanks stocked full of live ones year-round and priced very competitively, so you're always guaranteed high quality and good value from this place whenever you're in the market for some red guys. They also pick lots of fresh lobster meat every day for sale in their retail store and for their wholesale business. (David's supplies many of the area restaurants with their seafood, including fresh-picked lobster meat for, what else? Lobster rolls!)

The interior of the store has a cavernous feel to it, with its concrete floor and its open back wall leading to the fish-processing and loading dock areas. It's a bustling operation with well-informed counter help running around, filling orders and answering questions. Be sure to check out the well-stocked glass case filled with fish fillets (including spicy Cajun codfish fillets), fresh shellfish of all sorts, and prepared foods like crab cakes, cooked shrimp, and fresh-picked crabmeat. Much of the product on display is seasonal and locally sourced, which means it's as fresh as can be.

Before leaving with your order in hand, be sure to peruse the shelves lining two of the store's walls, where you'll find a wide variety of seafood complements, such as cocktail sauce (including Fabulous Franko's Wasabi Cocktail Blaze), various brands of hot sauces, and all sorts of interesting breadings and toppings to tart up your fish before baking. David's fun-loving staff will win you over, and their fresh seafood will keep you coming back for more.

David's Lobster Pie

David's Fish Market and Lobster Pound, Salisbury, Massachusetts

---

1 pound fresh-picked lobster meat

¾ sleeve Ritz crackers

½ cup Cheez-It crackers

4 tablespoons (½ stick) butter, plus
    3–4 pats

1 teaspoon garlic powder

1 teaspoon dried parsley

Grated Parmesan cheese (optional)

This is a simple recipe for a baked lobster dish that's rich with butter and lobster meat. It's a bit unusual in that it calls for two different types of crackers in its breading. Cracker variety is, after all, the spice of lobster life!

Preheat the oven to 400 degrees. Cut the lobster meat into bite-size pieces, and place into a casserole dish that has been lightly sprayed with vegetable oil.

Put the Ritz and Cheez-It crackers in a large Zip-Lock bag. Seal the bag, then crush the contents, using a rolling pin, until the crackers are reduced to crumbs and well mixed.

Melt the butter in a medium-size bowl in the microwave. Remove the bowl from the microwave and add the cracker crumbs, garlic, and parsley to the melted butter. Mix the combination well and pour over the lobster meat, then place a few more pats of butter on the top. Bake uncovered for 10 to 12 minutes, until the top turns golden brown. Sprinkle with Parmesan cheese, if desired. Serves 3 to 4.

Suggestion: You may substitute shrimp or chopped sea scallops for lobster meat. Don't skimp on the butter.

Lobster Benedict

Blount Market, Warren, Rhode Island

4 English muffins, toasted

1 bunch asparagus, blanched, trimmed, and halved on an angle

8 eggs, poached

4 lobster tails, shelled and halved

2 16-ounce containers of Legal Sea Foods Lobster Bisque

2 tablespoons fresh parsley, finely chopped

This oh-so-rich recipe calls for cans of lobster bisque from Legal Sea Foods (Blount's parent company manufactures the bisque for Legal), but any canned (or made-from-scratch) lobster bisque will do the trick. You may want to try the bisque from your local seafood market's refrigerated case.

Place the toasted English muffin halves in 8 separate shallow bowls. Blanch the asparagus, and arrange 3 to 4 pieces of asparagus on each muffin. Carefully place the poached eggs on top of the asparagus stalks. Add half a lobster tail to each. Ladle ¼ cup of lobster bisque over the top of each muffin, and sprinkle with fresh parsley. Serves 8.

Baked Stuffed Lobster

David's Fish Market and Lobster Pound, Salisbury, Massachusetts

2 1½-pound parboiled male lobsters (no eggs)

½ cup (1 stick) butter, divided

¾ sleeve Ritz crackers

½ cup Cheez-It crackers

½ pound sea scallops, chopped; or cleaned shrimp, chopped; or a mixture of both

1 tablespoon Worcestershire sauce (optional)

2 teaspoons garlic powder

2 teaspoons dried parsley

This embarrassment of shellfish riches is the signature dish at David's Fish Market. Numerous customers ask for this well-known recipe, especially around the holidays. Everyone at the market knows this is Dave's favorite!

Preheat the oven to 375 degrees. Parboil the lobsters (approximately 5 minutes). Remove the lobsters from the pot, let them cool, place them shell side down on a cutting board, and split them up the middle with a large, sharp knife (you may want to have your seafood market do this part for you).

Melt ½ stick of butter in a large bowl in the microwave. Crush the crackers in a large Zip-Lock bag (a rolling pin applied enthusiastically works well for this). Add the scallops/shrimp, Worcestershire sauce, garlic powder, dried parsley, and the cracker crumbs to the melted butter, and mix to a stuffing-like consistency.

Place the prepared lobsters on cookie sheets, shell sides down. Open them up, and fill them with the stuffing, using your hands to shape it into place. Don't pack it in too tightly, or it won't cook through. Slice the rest of the butter into pats, and place on top of the stuffing.

Bake for 15 minutes, or until the stuffing starts to turn golden brown, and serve. Melt extra butter for dipping the lobster meat, if desired. Serves 2.

Lobster or Crabmeat Quiche

Trenton Bridge Lobster Pound, Trenton, Maine

4 ounces grated cheddar cheese

4 ounces grated Swiss cheese

½ pound lobster meat or crabmeat
  (cut into bite-size pieces)

4 large eggs

3 cups milk

¾ teaspoon salt

1 tablespoon onion, minced

½ teaspoon dry mustard

2 tablespoons flour

This unique, cheese-heavy quiche recipe doesn't call for a pie crust of any sort, though you may use one as a base, if you wish. Quiche is a heartwarming comfort food, and it's made all the more so with fresh-picked lobster or crab-meat and lots of cheese.

Preheat the oven to 400 degrees. Line a large pie plate with the grated cheese. Add the chopped lobster meat (or crabmeat) on top of the cheese. In a medium-size bowl, beat the eggs, milk, salt, onion, mustard, and flour together. Pour over the seafood and cheese. Bake 10 minutes at 400 degrees, then another 40 minutes at 350 degrees. Let cool for 15 minutes before serving. Serves 4.

Port Clyde Lobster Pot Pie

Port Clyde Fresh Catch, Port Clyde, Maine

1½ cups yellow onion, chopped

¾ cup fennel, chopped

½ cup (1 stick) unsalted butter

½ cup all-purpose flour

2½ cups fish stock or clam juice

1 tablespoon Pernod

1½ teaspoons kosher salt

¾ teaspoon ground black pepper

3 tablespoons heavy cream

¾ pound cooked fresh lobster

1½ cups frozen peas

1½ cups frozen small whole onions

½ cup parsley, minced

CRUST

3 cups flour

1½ teaspoons salt

1 teaspoon baking powder

8 tablespoons fresh lard

8 tablespoons cold unsalted butter

½ to ⅔ cup ice water

1 egg, beaten with 1 tablespoon water or heavy cream, for egg wash

This lobster pie recipe from the good folks at Port Clyde Fresh Catch Fish Cooperative is more complicated than most, especially with the homemade crust. You may simplify it by using store-bought pie crusts and toppings. If you go the store-bought route, be prepared to have enough crust for two pies, which means twice the pleasure from this Mid-Coast Maine dish.

Sauté the onions and fennel with the butter in a large sauté pan on medium heat until the onions are translucent, about 10 to 15 minutes. Add the flour, and cook on low heat for 3 more minutes, stirring occasionally. Slowly add the stock, Pernod, salt, and pepper, and simmer for 5 more minutes. Then add the heavy cream.

Cut the lobster meat into bite-size chunks. Place the lobster, frozen peas, frozen onions, and parsley in a bowl. Pour the sauce over the mixture, and check the seasonings. Set the pan aside while you make the pastry crust.

For the crust, mix the flour, salt, and baking powder in a food processor fitted with a metal blade. Add the lard and butter and pulse 10 times, until the fat is the size of peas. With the motor running, add the ice water. Process only enough to moisten the dough and have it just come together. Dump the dough out on a floured surface and knead quickly into a ball. Wrap the dough in plastic and allow it to rest for 30 minutes in the refrigerator.

Preheat the oven to 375 degrees. Divide the dough in half and roll out each half to fit a 9-inch-round, 2-inch-deep baking dish. Place one rolled-out crust in the dish, and fill

with the lobster mixture. Top with the second crust. Crimp the crusts together around the edges with a fork, and brush the top with the egg wash. Make 4 to 5 slashes in the top crust to allow steam to escape during cooking, and bake for 1 hour and 15 minutes, until the top is golden brown and the filling inside is bubbling hot. Serves 6.

McLaughlin's Seafood

Bangor, Maine

Though Bangor, Maine, is some fifty miles from the open ocean, you wouldn't know it when you're at McLaughlin's Seafood. Just south of the downtown area and a stone's throw from the Penobscot River, McLaughlin's is always stocked with the finest fresh seafood products to be found in the upper reaches of Maine.

The McLaughlin family of Aroostook County, Maine, purchased the seafood market in 1978, and Reid McLaughlin in turn purchased the business from his father two years later. As other seafood markets in the area folded in the face of competition from supermarkets, McLaughlin's thrived, primarily because they sold fresh seafood to many of the Bangor-area restaurants. Over time, the retail market grew both in size and reputation, and it's now the best place in metro Bangor for fresh fish and shellfish.

Despite its inland location, McLaughlin's is every bit as fresh as what you'll find along the coast. They receive shipments from suppliers six days a week, and they drive their own truck down to Bass Harbor on Mount Desert Island and to Sorrento twice a week to buy seafood right off the boat from the fishermen there.

Housed in a whitewashed, cottage-like building with a red metal roof, McLaughlin's is easy to spot, with its angular red and white sign over the door and the large, red depiction of a lobster affixed to the front wall. Inside the market, you'll find an inviting glass case of such fresh fish fillets as haddock, swordfish, tuna, salmon, and sole. Fresh clams, oysters, shucked sea scallops, and jumbo shrimp are available for the most part year-round. And, of course, live lobster is a big seller here, for cooking at home. McLaughlin's will also package up and ship live lobsters anywhere in the country via FedEx Priority. There are a number of Maine-made products available on the shelves lining the walls, including whoopie pies,

Fieldstone Farm jams, and a complete line of Bar Harbor Foods canned products, such as chowders, bisques, and clams.

There are also a couple of dining options available at McLaughlin's. First is an adjoining seafood shack that serves up deep-fried seafood, chowders, stews, and lobster dinners on a seasonal basis. You can take your order to go or enjoy it at one of the picnic tables in front of the shack.

The other dining option is a couple of miles down the road in Hampden, right next to the Penobscot River. Called McLaughlin's at the Marina, it's a casual restaurant serving upscale food next to the banks of the river and Hamlin's Marina. Reid's wife, Kim, presides over the waterfront restaurant, where the menu is laden with fine seafood offerings as well as healthy salads and inventive pasta dishes.

With their year-round market and seasonal seafood shack and marina restaurant, the McLaughlins can say with certainty that they have the seafood waterfront covered in Bangor.

Lobster Mac 'n' Cheese

McLaughlin's Seafood, Bangor, Maine

1 pound macaroni noodles,
  uncooked

2 cups heavy cream

3 slices American cheese

2 slices Swiss cheese

3 ounces cheddar cheese,
  shredded

2 ounces blue cheese, crumbled

½ pound fresh-picked lobster meat
  (tail and knuckle), chopped
  into bite-size pieces

4 whole lobster claws, shelled

Here's a high-calorie, from-scratch version of this increasingly popular dish, featuring four different types of cheese. You may, of course, play with the types and proportions of cheeses in the mix, but this is actually a very compelling, stick-to-your-ribs approach that has many fans at McLaughlin's riverside restaurant in Hampden, Maine, coming back for more.

Bring a large pot of salted water to boil on the stovetop, and cook the macaroni according to instructions. Drain, rinse, and set aside in a large mixing bowl.

At the same time, in a medium-size saucepan over medium-low heat, slowly warm the cream until it starts to steam a bit. Add the cheeses, and stir or whisk until the cream and cheese are thoroughly combined.

Pour the cream-and-cheeses mixture over the cooked macaroni in the mixing bowl, blend in the chopped lobster meat, and mix gently but thoroughly. Spoon the macaroni mixture into four serving bowls, and top each one with a shelled lobster claw. Serves 4.

Tip: Sprinkle some panko over each of the servings, place the (oven-proof) bowls in a preheated 300-degree oven, and bake for 5 to 10 minutes until the tops get golden brown and crisp, then top each serving with a lobster claw. (Don't bake the claws on top. Put them on after the baking is complete.)

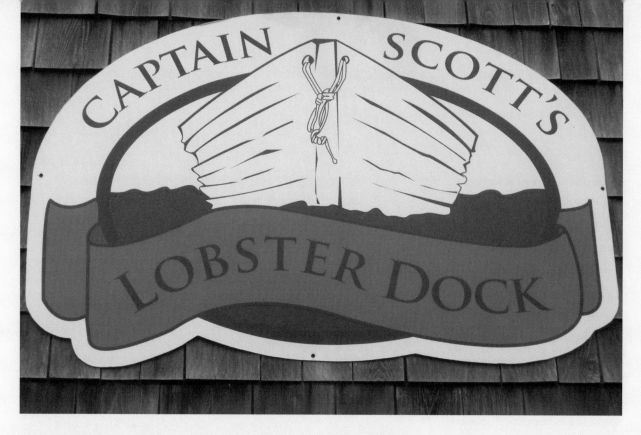

Captain Scott's Lobster Dock

New London, Connecticut

Captain Scott's is best known as one of the top seafood shacks in eastern Connecticut. Housed in a long, narrow-shingled, one-story building in the shadow of downtown New London, Connecticut, Captain Scott's sits on a thin strip of land between a commercial marina on Shaw's Cove and the Amtrak Acela train tracks. This improbable and seemingly impossible-to-find location is, however, crawling with seafood aficionados spring, summer, and fall, who find excellent fried, steamed, and boiled seafood delights.

There's also a nifty little seafood market in back of the seafood shack, accessible by a separate entrance, that offers a limited but high quality selection of fish and shellfish (including live lobster) that changes daily, depending on what's looking best and most available on a seasonal basis. Raw shrimp and fresh sea scallops are almost daily features, along with a few select varieties of whitefish fillets. Mussels and steamers are also available more often than not, and there's always fresh-picked lobster meat, in case you don't want to cook them yourself.

One taste treat not to be missed at this petite market is Tom's famous stuffed clams, referred to as "stuffies" here and at other seafood places in New England. A stuffie consists of minced clam meat blended with a poultry stuffing-type mixture and some form of chopped spicy sausage. The entire mixture is spooned into empty quahog clam shells and baked until cooked through. They make great appetizers or a nice snack any time of year.

SEAFOOD ROLLS AND SANDWICHES

Maine's Original Lobster Roll

Bayley's Lobster Pound, Scarborough, Maine

1 pound fresh lobster meat, cooked

⅓ cup real mayonnaise

5 hot dog rolls

Bayley's claims to be the originator of the lobster roll in Maine. Whether or not their claim is true (and we have no reason to doubt it), one thing is certain: this major player in the lobster business has a very simple and winning recipe for their version of the cold, Maine-style lobster roll, mixed with a little bit of mayo and a lot of love. Here it is.

Cut the lobster meat up into bite-size pieces. In a bowl, mix the lobster meat with the mayonnaise until all the meat is thoroughly coated. Fill the hot dog rolls with the lobster meat mixture. Serves 4 to 5.

Seafood Burgers

Atlantic Seafood, Old Saybrook, Connecticut

1 pound fish fillets

Seasoning (CharCrust seasoning is highly recommended)

¾ cup panko (more, if needed, to bind up properly)

These tasty seafood burgers from Atlantic Seafood may be made using salmon, swordfish, or tuna.

Grind the fillets in a meat grinder, or gently pulse them in a food processor to the consistency of ground meat. Add the seasoning and panko, and hand-knead until the burgers are thoroughly blended. Use enough panko to make the burgers bind up to the texture of a sticky, soft meatball. Form into 3 to 4 patties, and pan fry in 2 tablespoons of cooking oil, or cook on the grill until the patties are golden brown on the outside. Serves 3 to 4.

Flanders Fish Market

East Lyme, Connecticut

Back in late 1983, Paul and Donna Formica drove by a small house on a busy road in Flanders, Connecticut, and had an epiphany. "That would make a great spot for a fish market," thought Paul, and soon thereafter, with Donna pregnant with the first of their four children, Flanders Fish Market was born. After retrofitting the cottage to become a retail space, the Formicas had $41 left between them, which they used to make change from their cash register on opening day.

Flash forward more than thirty years, and Flanders Fish Market has grown into an eastern Connecticut institution, where people from Old Lyme to Stonington come for the freshest fish to be found on the eastern Connecticut shore. Flanders Fish has grown from a simple seafood market to a full-service restaurant and bar, banquet room, and demonstration kitchen. Yet its seafood-packed display cases remain the primary draw for folks in search of quality seafood.

One of the market's initial successes was its excellent clear-broth clam chowder (see the recipe on page 17), which was adapted from a local fisherman's recipe. Next came a request from a customer for fish and chips, which prompted the Formicas to purchase a deep fryer, and their food service business was off and running.

But the long-term key to Flanders's success is its beautifully stocked fresh seafood cases, front and center when you walk through the front door of the much expanded cottage, which has had a couple of additions and renovations over the years. Slabs of fresh-cut finned fish and buckets of fresh shellfish are on display, along with a case of tantalizing prepared seafood specialties, such as stuffed shrimp, crab cakes, mussel salad, smoked bluefish, herring in wine, seafood salad, and lobster pot pies.

The festive, colorful tile work on the walls and floor give Flanders a bit of a Mediterranean feel, and the friendly, knowledgeable staff behind the counter will dote on your every seafood need. In addition to carrying large supplies of the usual New England cornucopia of fish and shellfish species, Flanders also specializes in seasonal and special-order fish, such as blackfish, blue marlin, arctic char, mahimahi, shark, smelts, red snapper, shad and shad roe (a local favorite), grouper, and striped bass. If you don't see it in the cases, ask for it, and Flanders can special order virtually anything when it's in season.

One of the reasons for Flanders's longstanding success is the frequent trips made by refrigerated Flanders trucks to the Boston Fish Market, where they procure the freshest possible product. With Beantown only a couple hours away, these seafood shuttles are a vital lifeline to the retail business.

As if all this isn't enough, Flanders also has a unique "Demo Dining" setup, with a demonstration kitchen at one end of the restaurant's dining room. It's equipped with television cameras and screens around the dining room, so patrons may watch the chefs at work on Friday and Saturday evenings. Flanders also offers cooking classes and a unique "Captain's Table" experience, where groups are prepared a gourmet 5-course seafood meal in the demonstration kitchen.

All this from a humble, wood-frame cottage that, three decades ago, was minding its own business by the side of Chesterfield Road. Though Flanders Fish Market has grown dramatically over the years, you may still see the original cottage, which continues to face the street and put on a proud face for this cherished seafood mecca.

Hot Lobster Roll

Flanders Fish Market, East Lyme, Connecticut

¼ pound (1 stick) butter

3 tablespoons leeks, white part only, rinsed and minced (substitute with scallions)

3 tablespoons sherry (not cooking sherry)

1½ pounds fresh-picked lobster meat, cut into bite-size pieces

Coarse salt and fresh-ground black pepper, to taste

6 top-split hot dog rolls, buttered and toasted

1 lemon, cut into 6 wedges

Connecticut's version of the lobster roll is fresh-picked lobster meat bathed in warm, melted butter and served in a buttered, toasted, split-top New England hot dog roll. Flanders Fish Market has enhanced this simple recipe with a few minor variations of its own.

In a sauté pan over medium heat, melt the butter. Add the leeks and sauté for 2 minutes. Pour in the sherry, stir, and allow the mixture to meld by cooking for about 3 to 4 minutes.

Add the lobster meat to the pan, and sauté for 1 to 2 minutes, just enough to heat through. Season to taste with salt and pepper. Serve immediately in warm, toasted, buttered rolls, and garnish with lemon wedges. Serves 6.

Clam Shack Fried Clam Roll with Homemade Tartar Sauce

Clam Shack Seafood Market, Kennebunk, Maine

TARTAR SAUCE

1¼ cups mayonnaise

¼ cup drained sweet pickle relish

1 teaspoon dried onion powder

CLAM ROLLS

2 pints shucked, medium-size soft shell clams

½ cup milk

½ cup cold water

2 teaspoons clam liquor or bottled clam juice

1 cup flour

1 cup yellow corn flour (finely ground corn meal)

2 teaspoons salt

½ teaspoon black pepper

1–2 containers Crisco or other vegetable shortening

4 split-top hot dog rolls

3 tablespoons melted butter

Homemade tartar sauce (see above)

Lemon wedges

According to Clam Shack Seafood Market owner Steve Kingston, yes, you can fry clams at home! Be sure to use fresh, up-to-temperature oil, and eat the fried clams right away. And don't forget to make and chill the tartar sauce ahead of time.

Mix the tartar sauce ingredients together in a small bowl and refrigerate for at least two hours.

Trim off the clam necks, and rinse them if they're muddy. Combine the milk, water, and clam liquor in one bowl. Whisk together the flours, salt, and pepper in another bowl.

Using your clean hands, dip about ⅓ of the clams in the milk wash. Let the liquid drain off. Dredge the clams in the breading mix, making sure they are evenly coated. Transfer them to a colander, and shake off the excess flour mixture.

Heat the shortening over medium heat in a deep fryer or a heavy, deep skillet or pot until it melts and reaches 375 degrees. Carefully slide the clams into the fat, and deep fry until they're golden, about 1 to 2 minutes.

Using a slotted spoon, scoop out the fried clams and drain them on paper towels. Repeat with the remaining clams. (You can keep the first batches warm in a 200-degree oven for 10 to 15 minutes.)

At the same time, brush melted butter on the outsides of the hot dog rolls, and toast them on a medium-hot griddle or skillet until golden on both sides. Heap the fried clams into the toasted rolls, and serve with the tartar sauce and lemon wedges. Makes 4 clam rolls.

The Clam Shack Seafood Market

Kennebunk, Maine

This whitewashed seafood shack on the edge of the Kennebunk River in downtown Kennebunk is known for having what is widely believed to be the best lobster roll in all of Maine and New England, and, by extension, the world. Owner Steve Kingston has worked hard over the years to elevate the tiny eatery to international acclaim and has most likely succeeded beyond his wildest dreams.

What's less well known about the Clam Shack is its adjoining seafood market, with its limited but excellent selection of the day's catch from local fishermen and lobstermen who service the place during its May-to-October season. (One of their lobstermen is 97 years old!) What's also less known is that the seafood market was there first, and the eatery grew out of it as an add-on in 1968. Together, they make a wonderful pair—one-stop shopping for fresh and prepared seafood delights for take-home or dining at the shack.

A seafood market on this spot dates back to the late 1930s, and may be the longest continuously operated seafood market in the state. Originating with the Shackford family, the market became known as Shackford & Gooch when Bernice Shackford married Byron Gooch. Three generations of Shackfords and Gooches owned and ran the fish market until the mid-1980s. In 1968 the Jacques family began renting the Clam Shack and eventually bought the shack and seafood market in 1992. Steve and Jeni Kingston bought the operation from the Jacques in 2000 and have owned it ever since.

Though the Clam Shack is the better known of the two businesses, the seafood market is no slouch when it comes to fresh fish. Buying almost exclusively from local suppliers, the market carries a limited inventory of super-fresh seafood that's turned over daily. What doesn't sell in the market the day it arrives goes to the shack to be fried up and served in sandwiches, lunch boxes, and pint-size containers. The fresh seafood typically for sale in the market includes lobster (there's a large tank for viewing right next to the counter), haddock, salmon, scallops, and steamer clams. Also on hand is the market's "presidential-quality" swordfish, available whenever the nearby family of President George H. W. Bush wants to grill some up (see the recipe for Presidential Swordfish on page 97). You may buy some of this prized inventory for your own cookouts, if you wish.

Though most of the prepared dishes are served at the adjacent Clam Shack, the market offers the Fish Market Special—a cooked and cracked lobster with melted butter and potato chips. Take it home or enjoy it at one of several dining tables in the market itself (the market serves as an overflow spot of sorts for the Clam Shack, with open seating, a small gifts concession, and beer and wine on tap). If you decide to stay and eat, be sure to check out the live "StriperCam" feed on the television screen on the wall. There's an underwater camera mounted on a piling beneath the market that surveys the river bottom, where striped bass cruise the waters, waiting for people to drop them treats like oyster crackers from above. There are also a bunch of outdoor lobster-trap tables with benches on one side of the market, which makes for a great spot to dine and people-watch.

Though it lives in the shadow of the almighty Clam Shack, the Clam Shack Seafood Market should be at the top of your list for fresh seafood (and certainly fresh lobster) when visiting the Kennebunk area.

The Clam Shack Lobster Roll

Clam Shack Seafood Market, Kennebunk, Maine

Four 1-pound lobsters (the Clam Shack usually opts for soft-shell lobsters when they're available)

Melted butter

White bread rolls (a hot dog bun is traditional, but the Clam Shack uses a handmade, hamburger-style bakery roll)

Mayonnaise of your choice

Here it is, the recipe for the finest lobster roll in the world! The Clam Shack Seafood Market's adjoining seafood shack has won numerous awards and accolades from food writers and critics (and thousands of loyal customers) for its amazingly delectable cold lobster roll, and now you can make it at home. It's actually quite simple. One of the most important factors is the freshness of the ingredients.

Boil the lobsters in saltwater for 15 minutes. Remove them from the water, and set them aside to cool down.

Crack and pick the lobster tail, knuckle, and claw meat. Melt a bit of butter in a skillet, and grill the rolls, cut side down until golden. Smear on a bit of mayo, and pile the meat on the buns. Drizzle a bit of melted butter over the lobster, and serve with a lemon slice. Makes 4 lobster rolls.

Al's Seafood

North Hampton, New Hampshire

This place leads a dual life as a seafood shack on one side of its blue wooden building and a fully stocked seafood market on the other. Al's is on U.S. 1, about two miles northwest of tourist-crazy Hampton Beach (home of the annual Hampton Beach Seafood Festival), so it's well positioned to service the area's seafood-hungry crowds.

Al's has been in existence for over twenty years. It was founded by Al Courchene after he purchased a small seafood market and began building a following with his fresh seafood offerings and his skills in the kitchen. The business grew over the years, with Al eventually replacing the outdoor picnic tables with a new indoor dining area, enabling him to become a year-round establishment.

Lobsters are a popular item here, both whole and in lobster roll form. Al's will be happy to cook up your lobsters or steamers for take-out. They will also refrigerate your seafood order and ship it overnight anywhere in the country, if you wish. Other shellfish standouts include mussels, littleneck clams, and oysters from Maine, squid from Rhode Island, and a wide variety of raw or cooked shrimp from Mexico.

Finned fish selections include haddock and sole from various parts of New England, swordfish and halibut from Canada, cod from Gloucester, salmon from Scotland, tuna and mahimahi from Mexico, and sea bass from Chile.

Two of the standout prepared foods in Al's seafood market are homemade fish cakes and stuffed haddock, both ready to take home and heat up for an instant dinner. Much of the rest of the market's space is given over to fresh produce in season, such as broccoli, bell peppers, cucumbers, zucchini, summer squash, and corn on the cob. A large, stained-glass-style art piece of a colorful mahimahi hangs over the produce bins, putting customers in the mood for fresh, healthy seafood.

The order counter for the seafood shack is in a back corner of the market, with chalkboards announcing the various lobster options, baked, grilled, or sautéed dinners, seafood rolls and sandwiches, and fried seafood platters. Order at the counter, then retire to the dining room in the attached addition next door, and wait for your number to be called.

All in all, Al's has everything you need in the way of seafood, fresh or cooked, all within a short drive of beautiful, bustling Hampton Beach.

The Hampton Beach Seafood Festival

Each September, on the weekend following Labor Day, the seaside town of Hampton Beach, New Hampshire, rolls out the red carpet for one of the largest and most fun seafood festivals in New England.

The Hampton Beach Seafood Festival got its start in the late 1980s, when a group of Hampton-area merchants and restaurateurs decided to put on a waterfront festival to promote local businesses and seafood. After a slow start, the festival grew over the years, eventually taking over the entire downtown area of Hampton Beach, with large tents and entertainment venues set up on the waterfront to house all the food, live music, and other goings on.

Today the festival draws nearly 150,000 people over its three-day duration. There are food booths featuring area restaurants and specialty food purveyors (mostly seafood), a beachside stage where live music plays throughout the festival, culinary chef demos, a "kiddieland" tent, fireworks, and a lobster-roll-eating contest.

But the big draw is the food, and there's plenty of it. It's a great way to sample lots of the local fare (especially lobster!) and to spend some time outdoors in sun and sand before the winds of autumn begin to blow. www.hamptonbeachseafoodfestival.com

SALMON, SWORDFISH, AND TUNA

Oven Roasted Salmon

Atlantic Seafood, Old Saybrook, Connecticut

1–2 pounds salmon fillets

1 tablespoon olive oil

Juice of 1 lemon

¼ cup dry white wine

It doesn't get much simpler or easier than this salmon recipe from Atlantic Seafood in Old Saybrook. That's probably why it tastes so good.

Preheat the oven to 350 degrees. Place the fillets in a baking dish and brush with olive oil. Add the lemon juice and wine to the baking dish, and cover lightly with waxed paper or aluminum foil. Bake for 20 minutes. Serves 2 to 4.

Tip: Any sort of dill topping goes well with this dish. See Atlantic Seafood's dill topper recipe on page 258.

Jim's Swordfish

Sanders Fish Market, Portsmouth, New Hampshire

¼ cup Hellmann's mayonnaise

½ teaspoon dried dill weed

½ teaspoon dried tarragon

½ teaspoon dried basil

Juice of ¼–½ lemon, to taste

2 pounds swordfish (1 inch thick)

This recipe comes from Jim Sanders, a founder of the family's fish market and father of current owner Mike Sanders. It's a simple recipe (most of the good ones are), and you may cook the fish under the broiler or on the grill.

In a small bowl, whisk together the mayonnaise, herbs, and lemon juice. Set aside for 10 minutes or so to let the flavors combine. Pat both sides of the swordfish with a paper towel to dry.

Spread the mayonnaise mixture on both sides of the swordfish, and place the fish on a broiler pan beneath the preheated broiler or directly on the preheated grill. Broil or grill for 4 to 5 minutes per side, until the fish flakes slightly with the insertion of a fork. Serves 4.

Seaport Fish

Rye, New Hampshire

Just south of Portsmouth, New Hampshire, on Route 1A in the seaside town of Rye, sits Seaport Fish, which has been in business since 1978. Serving up lots of local and regional fish and shellfish from the local docks and the docks of Boston and Portland, Maine, Seaport Fish is owned and run by Rich Pettigrew, and has stood the test of time in a crowded New Hampshire seafood market. These days, it remains a favorite among many locals and summertime residents.

Housed in a varnished-wood clapboard, one-story building with red metal roof and lots of maritime kitsch scattered out front, this homey market exudes good vibes, from its well-stocked seafood cases to its copious bins of fresh produce to its refrigerated and frozen gourmet food items. Add to that the knowledgeable staff, and you've got a great place to pick up everything you need to make a healthy, seafood-based lunch or dinner.

Rich and his team do all that they can to procure their product from local fishermen, primarily out of Portsmouth,

Rye, Hampton, and Seabrook, New Hampshire, to support the local fishing communities and to stock the freshest possible product. They have direct relationships with numerous day boats, which in turn rely on Seaport Fish for a lot of their profits.

Among the great seafood to be found within the market are such items as mako shark (great for grilling), wild-caught bluefish (in season), sole, haddock, and monkfish, along with an array of wild-caught shrimp of varying sizes, many of them from the Gulf of Mexico. Farm-raised and wild-caught salmon are featured nearly year-round, next to local swordfish and richly colored, finely textured slabs of tuna.

Many area restaurants buy their fish from Seaport, a testament to the quality of the product that Rich and his crew serve up on a daily basis. Stop in and load up your basket for your next seafood adventure, if you happen to be in this lovely corner of the Granite State.

Bud's Sesame Ahi Tuna

Bud's Fish Market, Branford, Connecticut

2 pounds ahi tuna, cut into 4
portions, 1½ inches thick

¼ cup avocado oil

¼ cup black sesame seeds

1 pound seaweed salad

Here's a simple and effective way to enjoy tuna steaks without employing the grill—particularly appealing during the colder months of the year.

Rub the tuna steaks lightly on both sides with the avocado oil. Cover with sesame seeds, and lightly pat the seeds into the flesh of the fish.

Heat a large skillet on the stovetop until hot. Pan sear the tuna in the hot skillet, only 1 minute per side for medium rare. Serve on top of a bed of seaweed salad. Serves 4.

Baked, Broiled Swordfish Dijon

City Fish Market, Wethersfield, Connecticut

½ cup mayonnaise (it's OK to use
   light mayo, if you wish)

2 tablespoons Dijon mustard

Juice of 1 lemon

2 pounds fresh swordfish steaks

Salt and pepper to taste

Swordfish is always plentiful at City Fish Market in Wethersfield, Connecticut, and it's also very competitively priced. It's no wonder they like to share this recipe with their customers, who count on City Fish for a steady supply of this meaty, highly versatile fish steak—whether it's cooked in the oven or thrown on the grill.

Preheat the oven to 400 degrees. Combine the mayonnaise, Dijon mustard, and lemon juice in a small bowl. Put the swordfish steaks on a broiler pan, and season both sides with salt and pepper. Spread half of the mayo mixture over the top of the swordfish, place the pan on the middle rack of the oven, and bake for 5 to 6 minutes. Turn the fish over and spread the remaining mayo mixture over the fish. Return to the oven and bake for another 4 to 5 minutes.

Remove the fish from the oven and set aside. Set the oven to broil, and move the oven rack closer to the heat source. Watching closely, broil the fish just until topping is lightly charred. Serves 4.

Variation: You may use this topping and grill the swordfish steaks on your gas or charcoal grill outside.

Seared Tuna

Atlantic Seafood, Old Saybrook, Connecticut

1 tablespoon olive oil

1½ to 2 pounds ahi tuna

Char Crust brand dry rub seasoning (Char Crust Ginger Teriyaki or Smoky Spicy Southwest rubs work best with tuna)

Heat the olive oil in a pan over medium heat until it's almost smoking. Thoroughly season the tuna on all sides with Char Crust dry rub. Sear the tuna on top, bottom, and all sides for 30 seconds each. Set the tuna aside to cool. Slice the tuna thin with a sharp knife, cutting against the grain. Serves 4.

Tip: Serve on a bed of seaweed salad with a ponzu dipping sauce.

Sweet and Spicy Sriracha-Glazed Salmon

Nauset Fish and Lobster Pool, Orleans, Massachusetts

¼ cup reduced-sodium soy sauce

2 tablespoons honey

1 tablespoon rice vinegar

1 tablespoon sriracha (more or
    less, to taste)

1 tablespoon fresh ginger, grated

1 tablespoon garlic, minced

1 pound wild king salmon fillet,
    cut into two pieces

1½ teaspoons sesame oil

The spicy, flavorful sriracha of Thai origin livens up this dish's sauce, which is a great complement to fresh, wild king salmon fillets.

In a one-gallon Ziplock bag, combine the soy sauce, honey, rice vinegar, sriracha, ginger, and garlic. Put the salmon in the bag, zip the bag shut, and shake lightly until the two fillets are coated. Refrigerate for at least 1 hour, to let the flavors soak into the fillets.

Heat the sesame oil in a skillet over medium high heat. Brown the salmon pieces in the skillet, about 2 minutes per side. Pour the remaining marinade into the pan over the salmon, reduce the heat to low, cover the pan, and cook until the salmon is cooked through, approximately 4 to 5 minutes. Serves 2.

Sautéed Yellowtail Tuna

Kyler's Catch Seafood Market, New Bedford, Massachusetts

4 yellowtail tuna fillets,
approximately ⅓–½ pound
each

1 cup fish-fry breading mix

2 tablespoons olive oil

2 tablespoons butter

1 lemon, cut into wedges

¼ cup parsley, finely chopped

With the breaded coating, this is a foolproof way to cook tuna without drying it out.

Dredge the fillets in the breading mix. Heat the olive oil and butter together in a skillet over high heat. Place the fillets in the skillet, and cook 4–5 minutes per side until crispy and golden brown. Serve with lemon wedges and parsley for garnish. Serves 4.

Kyler's Seafood

New Bedford, Massachusetts

New Bedford is the one of the largest fishing ports in the United States, and Kyler's Seafood is the largest retail fish market in town. You can bet that the seafood is fresh and plentiful at all times in Kyler's showy retail store, just off I-195 on the edge of the city. It's the perfect place to pull off and grab some fish on your way to or from nearby Cape Cod.

Kyler's roots go back to the 1930s, when a man in Newark, New Jersey, named Alfred Nanfelt, started selling fish out of his garage under the name of Coastal Fisheries. After several years of expansion in the New York, New Jersey, Philadelphia, and Baltimore markets, the company moved to New Bedford in 1946, where it has been a major player in the seafood-processing and distribution businesses ever since.

Jeff Nanfelt, the third generation of the family to be involved in the business, became president in the 1980s and renamed the business Kyler Seafoods in 1985. Ten years later, Nanfelt opened a gourmet retail market on one side of the massive processing plant, and thus was born Kyler's Catch Seafood Market.

Kyler's is quite a sight from the road, with its stark, bright, sea-blue and aquamarine façade and large rooftop sign, beckoning drivers to pull off I-195 for a closer inspection. It's even more impressive after you walk up the short flight

of outside stairs and step into the marketplace. Before you is a virtual hallway running from right to left of glassed, refrigerated seafood cases, decked out across the bottom with bright, cheery ceramic tile, inviting you to stroll down the hall and take in all the seafood delights on display.

Being a major player in the seafood-processing business, Kyler's is particularly strong in its prepared seafood offerings. Among the array of regularly featured items are fresh stuffed salmon, stuffed Alaskan cod, baked stuffed shrimp, tortilla-crusted tilapia, and chipotle lemon swordfish kabobs. There is also a wide variety of cooked shrimp of various sizes, 30-ounce containers of fresh-made New England–style clam chowder, and ready-made clam bakes in foil-sealed trays for heating up on the stovetop or grill.

The fresh seafood case is no slouch here, either. There are mounds of Alaskan cod fillets and tails, tilapia, salmon steaks, halibut, haddock, Arctic char, swordfish, tuna, squid tubes, and whole rainbow trout. Fresh sea scallops and previously frozen diver's scallops join a variety of clams, oysters, and fresh-picked crab and lobster meat in the lineup.

Speaking of lobsters, there's a large lobster tank anchoring one end of the seafood hall, where you may pick out your own from the tank, which resembles a miniature, tile-fringed swimming pool.

Kyler's is definitely the place to shop for fresh and gourmet prepared seafood when you're in New Bedford, and it's perfect for easy-off, easy-on shopping when touring the Cape and other waterfront spots in southeastern Massachusetts.

Kyler's Roasted Salmon

Kyler's Catch Seafood Market, New Bedford, Massachusetts

1–1½ pounds thick salmon fillets (skinned)

1 teaspoon garlic powder

2 tablespoons Blue Crab Bay seafood herbs

4 tablespoons olive oil, divided

1 pint cherry tomatoes

1 large Vidalia or other sweet onion, cut into thin wedges

Here's a unique and wonderful way to roast fresh salmon, which uses both the stovetop and the oven and throws in some fresh tomatoes and onion wedges for good measure.

Preheat the oven to 350 degrees. Cut the salmon into 4-inch-wide pieces. Mix the garlic powder and seafood herbs together, and sprinkle half on the fillets.

Heat 1 tablespoon of olive oil in an oven-safe frying pan. Sauté the salmon for 3 minutes on each side, then remove from heat. Combine the remaining olive oil and garlic/seafood herbs mixture in a large bowl, add the cherry tomatoes and onion wedges, and mix together.

Arrange the tomato/onion mixture around the salmon fillets while the fillets are still in the pan. Roast the salmon in the pan in the preheated oven for 12 minutes. Serves 3 to 4.

Champlin's Seafood

Narragansett, Rhode Island

This fresh-seafood mecca in southern Rhode Island is about as close to the source as you can get in the seafood market business. Every day, numerous boats pull up to the Galilee docks behind Champlin's and offload a wide variety of fish and shellfish from near and far. It's only several yards from the loading zone to the display cases in the market, and what isn't shipped out to retail customers such as restaurants and grocery stores finds its way to the lucky customers who come through Champlin's doors seven days a week, year-round.

Champlin's seafood market occupies the first floor of a two-story multipurpose building that also houses a famous dine-in-the-rough restaurant and bar on the second floor and a small ice cream shop at ground level. It's just a couple hundred yards from the Block Island Ferry terminal, through which thousands of passengers pass every day on their way to the fabled island several miles offshore.

The seafood market first opened in 1932, purchasing its inventory from the local fishing boats and selling it to locals and tourists in search of fresh fish and shellfish. Retailing led to wholesaling (it usually goes the other way), and Champlin's presence on the Galilee docks (home to Rhode Island's largest commercial fishing fleet) grew over the years. Champlin's has been a longtime supplier of such stellar East Coast fish markets as the Fulton Market in Manhattan (now in the Bronx) and the famed Fish Pier in Boston.

At various times in the past, Champlin's has had a dedicated fishing fleet servicing its retail and wholesale businesses. Take a walk around the exterior of the building and you'll notice a bunch of lifesaving ring buoys nailed to the façade. Each buoy bears the name of a boat that has at one time or another sailed and fished as part of Champlin's exclusive fleet of fishing vessels.

There's nothing slick about the presentation at Champlin's; just old-school fish mongering in the best sense. Overhead, fluorescent-tube lighting lends the market an instant nostalgic feel. There are two glassed-in seafood cases straight ahead, flanked by open-air tables covered with a variety of whole fish and shellfish on beds of crushed ice. On any given day, you may find fresh whole flounder, hake, bluefish, squid (the port of Galilee takes in the largest quantity of squid in the United States), and whatever else is in season and in abundance.

The seafood cases offer glimpses of fresh filleted swordfish, halibut, flounder, cod, day-boat sea scallops, raw jumbo shrimp, and fresh, chopped sea clams for chowders, casseroles, and more. In the prepared seafood case, standout selections include smoked fish like mackerel and bluefish, calamari salad, mussel salad, and Champlin's famous snail salad, all marinating in tasty oil-and-vinegar dressings.

Champlin's has always prided itself as being the nexus of fresh whole lobster in the western portion of Narragansett Bay. The market sports several aquamarine tanks, one of which displays lobsters that customers may pick out and have sent upstairs to be cooked and eaten on Champlin's airy seafood deck, overlooking the harbor. But perhaps the crown jewel in the first-floor market is the tabletop display of fresh whole clams (chowders, cherrystones, littlenecks, and steamers), available by the pound or the bushel.

If ever there was a one-stop seafood shop that can handle all your seafood needs, Champlin's is the place to go.

Baked Salmon with Lemon Dill Sauce

Champlin's Seafood, Narragansett, Rhode Island

2 salmon fillets (approximately 1½ pounds)

¼ cup white wine, divided

Juice of 1 lemon, divided

Pinch of garlic powder

1 cup fish or chicken stock

1 tablespoon fresh dill, chopped

1 tablespoon cornstarch

1 tablespoon water

Preheat the oven to 350 degrees. Place the salmon fillets in a baking dish, top with splashes of white wine and lemon juice, and bake for 30 minutes or until the fish begins to flake. Remove the fish from the oven, set aside on a plate, and cover, reserving the drippings in the baking pan.

In a sauté pan, combine the salmon drippings and the stock, and bring to a boil. Flavor with white wine and garlic powder, and add lemon and dill to taste. Continue to reduce by boiling, and thicken to a gravy-like consistency by adding the cornstarch pre-mixed with the water until the desired consistency is achieved.

Serve the fillets on beds of rice with the lemon dill sauce poured on top. Serves 3 to 4.

STEWS AND CASSEROLES

Bud's Oyster Stew

Bud's Fish Market, Branford, Connecticut

1½ pints shucked oysters with liquid

2 tablespoons butter (¼ stick)

Salt and pepper to taste

1 quart milk

This is a great dish for cold winter evenings, with its capacity to warm and its taste of the sea.

Drain the oysters, strain, and reserve the liquid. Using a deep frying pan or shallow pot, sauté the oysters over medium heat with the butter until the edges curl slightly. Add salt and pepper to taste.

Add the reserved oyster liquid and milk to the pan. Heat until hot and steaming, but do not boil. Serve in bowls with oyster crackers or a loaf of fresh bread. Serves 4.

Codfish Casserole

City Fish Market, Wethersfield, Connecticut

2½ pounds boneless cod fillets

1 can (10½ ounces) condensed cream of shrimp soup

½ cup (1 stick) margarine or butter, melted

1 teaspoon Worcestershire sauce

1 teaspoon lemon juice

Dash Tabasco sauce

30 crushed crackers (use ½ Ritz and ½ unsalted soda crackers)

2 teaspoons parsley, chopped

This casserole will become a star in your seafood repertoire. City Fish Market recommends serving it with rice amandine, steamed Chinese peas, and some cranberry sauce on the side.

Preheat the oven to 400 degrees. Cut the fillets into serving-size pieces, and place them in a buttered, flat-bottomed casserole dish. Pour and spread the soup on top. Bake at 375 degrees for 15 minutes. While the fish is baking, mix the remaining ingredients. Remove the fish from the oven, spread the mixture over the fish, and continue baking for 8 to 10 minutes, or until the fish flakes easily with a fork.

Makes 6 servings.

Gardner's Wharf Seafood

Wickford, Rhode Island

Housed in a cedar-shingled building with wood-trimmed windows on a wharf in the charming seaside hamlet of Wickford, Rhode Island, Gardner's Wharf Seafood is just the kind of seafood market every coastal town in New England should have. With its open floor plan of display cases and its table-top offerings of shellfish and fresh vegetables, this western Rhode Island stalwart serves as a magnet for seafood lovers from Warwick to Narragansett.

Overlooking Wickford Harbor, Gardner's came to be in 2003 when owner Pete Chevalier took over the building on the wharf, which for a long stretch in its past had been a chowder house, and he outfitted it for retail seafood sales. Its location right next to the docks in Wickford made it an ideal spot to do business with the local fishermen on Narragansett Bay. Soon, clamming boats and other shellfishing operations made daily stops at Gardner's back-door wharf, offloading their catches for processing and sale.

Though shellfishing on Narragansett Bay isn't as robust as it once was, Gardner's is still the place to go in western Rhode Island for the biggest and best varieties of fresh clams and oysters. There's a wonderful display table in the store that showcases the clam catches of the day, where you can purchase clams by the piece, pound, or bushel. There are littlenecks, cherrystones, quahogs, mussels, and steamers in the clam category and a variety of locally harvested oysters from Narragansett Bay and nearby saltwater pond nurseries.

A good amount of the finned fish available at Gardner's is also offloaded at the back door, making it as fresh as can be. This includes striped bass and black sea bass in the summertime. Nonlocal fish, such as swordfish and Pacific salmon, are picked up regularly from the fish market in Boston, and Gardner's has a special buyer in not-too-distant New Bedford, Massachusetts, for daily procurements of flounder and cod.

The star of the prepared foods case at Gardner's is the array of stuffed clams, or "stuffies," as they're referred to in Rhode Island. These delectable hors d'oeuvre-like treats consist of minced clams blended with breaded stuffing, sausage, and spices, all lumped into individual quahog shells. You may have your stuffies plain, spicy, or "gourmet" at Gardner's, and there's Pete's special Stuffed Scallops. Clam chowders in the refrigerated cases include creamy white, tomato red, and Rhode Island clear broth varieties.

Live lobster is available year-round, and you may pick your own from the tank that lines one side of the display room. Another treat to keep in mind is the Gardner's Wharf "Clambakes to Go." Each individual clambake comes in a reusable steel pot with a sealing lid and includes a 1¼-pound lobster, a pound each of steamers and mussels, a sausage wrapped in a flounder fillet, potatoes, corn, carrots, and onion. Just add water and steam to perfection on your stovetop or outdoor grill.

Grandma David's Famous Seafood Casserole

David's Fish Market and Lobster Pound, Salisbury, Massachusetts

3 tablespoons milk

1 pound haddock fillets (skinless or skin on, either way works)

2 tablespoons mayonnaise

4–6 slices American cheese (optional)

½ pound sea scallops

½ pound raw shrimp, peeled

1 cup Cheez-It crackers

1 sleeve Ritz crackers

½ cup (1 stick) butter, divided

2–3 teaspoons garlic powder

2–3 teaspoons dried parsley

The grandmother of current owner Gordon Blaney used to serve this wonderful seafood casserole to her family back in the mid-1900s. It has stood the test of time and is still a favorite with the Blaney clan.

Preheat the oven to 375 degrees. Spray a 9 × 12-inch baking dish with Pam or other vegetable oil spray.

Spoon the milk into the baking dish, and put the haddock fillets on top of the milk. (If the skin is still on, place the skin side down.) Spread the mayonnaise on the fillets, then place the cheese slices on top, followed by the scallops and shrimp.

Crush the Ritz and Cheez-It crackers in a large, sealed Zip-Lock bag, using a rolling pin or other method of crushing. Melt half the stick of butter in a large bowl in the microwave, then add the crushed crumbs, garlic powder, and parsley flakes to the melted butter and blend thoroughly. Spread the cracker mixture evenly over the top of the seafood. Cut the rest of the butter into pats, and place them on top of the crumb mixture. (Don't skimp on the butter. It keeps the seafood moist and flavorful.)

Cover the dish with foil and bake for 30 minutes in the preheated oven. Uncover and bake for another 10 to 15 minutes, or until golden brown. Use a fork and check for large, moist flakes of haddock, indicating that the casserole is ready. Serves 4 to 5.

Browne Trading Market

Portland, Maine

Of the three major seafood markets on the Portland waterfront (Harbor Fish, Browne, and Free Range), Browne is definitely the most gourmet of the bunch, with its priceless inventory of caviar from around the world, its extensive offerings of seafood smoked on the premises, and its cavernous wine shop with thousands of bottles to peruse. But it's also a seafood market that offers plenty of fresh fish and shellfish from the nearby docks at Merrill's Wharf and beyond.

The Browne's story dates back to the early 1800s, when John Brown (the "e" was added to the family name during the Civil War) took up catching and selling fish from his home on the Kennebec River, north of Brunswick. Caviar harvested from the sturgeon in the river became a Brown specialty.

Several generations later, in 1979, Rod Browne Mitchell opened a wine and cheese shop in Camden. Mitchell had two passions: gourmet food and wine and a love for fishing and the sea, which was passed on to him by his grandfather. Rod began carrying caviar in his shop and eventually began supplying Maine diver scallops and peekytoe crabmeat to famous chefs in high-end restaurants in Manhattan and other East Coast cities.

In 1991, Rod and his wife relocated Browne to Merrill's Wharf on the Portland waterfront, where the business really took off as a first-rate trader in caviar, a wholesaler of fish from around the world, and a supplier of top-shelf seafood to a select group of world-famous chefs and restaurants. In 1995, Browne began smoking all its own seafood on premises, and in 2000, Browne Trading Market, an upscale retail seafood market and wine shop, opened its doors.

The seafood market is a very special place, housed in the brick storefront of the larger Browne operation, which is in back and next door. The beautifully designed and appointed market has exposed brick walls and a white ceramic tile floor in an open, high-ceilinged, split-level room. On the main floor are the seafood cases, stocked with filleted and whole fish and shellfish, as well as a select offering of Browne's famous caviar (most of the caviar is kept in the deep recesses of the large building adjacent to the market). Also on the ground floor are shelves and refrigerator cases filled with gourmet foods and cheeses, as well as cauldrons of hot soups and stews for the take-out lunch crowd.

Browne smokes virtually all its own fish on the premises and even employs what is known as a "smokemaster" to oversee the entire smoking operation. There is a variety of smoked salmon, either thin-sliced or whole fillets, along with smoked trout, finnan haddie (smoked haddock), and smoked shrimp, mussels, and sea scallops.

Walk up a short flight of stairs from the market, and you'll find yourself in one of the finest wine shops in Portland. There are thousands of bottles in wooden racks and on tabletops—wines of all types, vintages, and price ranges. Seasonal wines are also stocked next to the seafood cases downstairs, but the motherlode is in the upstairs cellar.

Browne is a great spot to stock up on all sorts of exotic seafood fare, and it's also an excellent choice for everyday cuts of fish that are a cut above what you'll find in most other places. And if you're in the market for some world-class caviar, there's no better place to be.

Italian Fisherman's Stew

Browne Trading Market, Portland, Maine

2 fennel bulbs, medium diced

2 Spanish onions, finely diced

2 tablespoons olive oil

1 cup dry white wine

1 tablespoon dried thyme

1 tablespoon dried rosemary

6 cups fish stock

15 ounces crushed tomatoes

3 pounds local haddock, cod,
monkfish, or halibut

In a Dutch oven or other large, heavy-bottomed pot, sauté the fennel and onions in the olive oil over medium heat until softened, about 5 minutes. Turn the heat to high, and, once the pot is sizzling, add the white wine and deglaze, stirring constantly.

Add the thyme and rosemary, and simmer for 2 minutes. Add the fish stock and crushed tomatoes, and continue simmering until hot. Add the fish in whole fillets, cook through for a few minutes, break apart the fillets, and serve immediately. Serves 10.

Smoky Monkfish and Mussels Marinara

Mac's Seafood, Wellfleet, Massachusetts

¼ cup olive oil

1 sweet onion (one cup, chopped fine)

1 small shallot (2 tablespoons, minced)

6 garlic cloves, minced

1 teaspoon red pepper flakes

2 teaspoons smoked pimentón (sweet paprika from Spain)

2–3 sprigs fresh thyme (or 1 teaspoon dried thyme)

1 cup white wine

2 28-ounce cans whole tomatoes, in their juices

18 littleneck clams

18 mussels

This has to be one of the tastiest, most exotic seafood stews you'll encounter on Cape Cod or anywhere in New England. The combination of monkfish (otherwise known as poor man's lobster), clams, and mussels with a spicy, tomato-based stew is irresistible and makes a great feast for family and friends.

Warm the olive oil in a large Dutch oven or stew pot over medium heat. Add the minced onion, shallot, and garlic, and sauté gently for a minute or two until aromatic (don't let the aromatics brown, or they'll taste bitter). Stir in the red pepper flakes, the pimentón, and the thyme. Add the wine and simmer for just a minute, then add the tomatoes—juice and all—to form a stew. Break up the tomatoes if you're using the whole variety.

While the stew simmers for a few minutes longer, scrub the clams and mussels in cold water to remove any sand and grit. If the mussels have beards, firmly pull them against the shell

2¼ pounds monkfish fillets

Kosher or sea salt

Freshly ground black pepper

½ cup fresh parsley, minced

Crusty country bread, toasted

½ cup muhammara (roasted red pepper dip), optional

to cut them off. Trim the membranes off the monkfish fillets, cut them into big, thick medallions or chunks, and salt and pepper them generously.

Drop the clams into the pot first, to be followed by the monkfish. To build flavor with the monkfish, heat a skillet on the stove top, drizzle in a little olive oil, and sear the monkfish on one side, to get it nice and caramelized before you add it to the pot. (You may skip the searing, if you wish.)

Once the clams just begin to open, lay in the monkfish pieces and poke them down gently into the bubbling stew. Simmer for just a few minutes, then add the mussels. Keep things simmering until all the shellfish are open (discard any that don't open) and the monkfish is cooked up white and firm. Serve in big, wide bowls with minced parsley and toasty sliced bread on top. Serves 6.

Optional: Slather some muhammara on the bread slices before placing the bread on top of the stew.

Trenton Bridge Lobster Pound

Trenton, Maine

Along Route 3 in the town of Trenton, Maine, just before you get on the bridge that takes you to Mount Desert Island and Acadia National Park, you'll come across a most unusual sight—several wood-stoked cookers, each with a tin chimney belching wisps of woodsmoke into the air, and a line of hungry tourists waiting for their victuals to be boiled and served. Welcome to the Trenton Bridge Lobster Pound and seafood market.

Trenton Bridge Lobster Pound has been around since the mid-1950s and is a family-owned operation that's currently in its third and fourth generations. Lobster is the big draw here, whether cooked or live and packaged for take-away or shipment across the country. There are several other seafood offerings to consider, many of them in frozen form, that make for great purchases if you're planning on being in the area for a while.

Fresh steamers and mussels are available in season and make for great appetizers or entire meals in larger quantities. In the freezers of Trenton Bridge's store you'll find frozen lobster meat, crabmeat, sea scallops, and lobster tails. All are locally caught and available during Trenton Bridge's Memorial Day to Columbus Day season.

Keep this place in mind when you're vacationing in the Acadia area. It's a great spot for lunch or dinner out of the roadside cookers, or for great frozen seafood to stock in your rental kitchen or for transport home.

Scallop Casserole

Trenton Bridge Lobster Pound, Trenton, Maine

1 cup Ritz crackers, crushed into crumbs and divided into two equal portions

2 pounds sea scallops, cut into bite-size pieces

¼ teaspoon salt

Rosemary to taste

⅛ teaspoon black pepper

½ cup half-and-half or light cream

½ cup (1 stick) butter, cut into pats

Preheat the oven to 375 degrees. Coat the bottom of a casserole dish with a light spray of vegetable oil. Pour one half of the cracker crumbs in the bottom of the dish, followed by the scallops, then the remainder of the cracker crumbs. Sprinkle the salt, rosemary, and pepper over the crumbs, pour the half-and-half or cream on top, then place the butter pats evenly over the top of everything.

Bake for 45 minutes. Remove from the oven, and allow to cool for 5 to 10 minutes before serving. Serves 5 to 6.

COD AND HADDOCK

Cappy's Cod

Flanders Fish Market, East Lyme, Connecticut

4 6-ounce cod fillets, rinsed and patted dry with paper towels (store in refrigerator if not using immediately)

2 tablespoons garlic, minced

2 tablespoons shallots, minced

2 tablespoons parsley, minced

2 sprigs thyme, leaves only

2 sprigs marjoram

2 stalks basil, leaves only, roughly chopped

Coarse salt and freshly ground black pepper, to taste

1 15-ounce can diced tomatoes, drained

½ cup breadcrumbs

4 tablespoons dry vermouth

½ cup water

1 lemon, cut into wedges

This is a delightfully gourmet way to prepare baked fresh cod. There is a symphony of herbs and spices that really make this dish come to life.

Preheat the oven to 450 degrees. Place the fillets in an 11 × 14-inch Pyrex or ovenproof baking dish or nonstick baking pan. Top each fillet with an equal amount of garlic and shallots, spreading them evenly over the fillets. Sprinkle each fillet with the parsley, thyme, marjoram, basil, salt, and pepper, distributing evenly.

Top the fillets with the tomatoes, distributing evenly, then top each fillet with an equal amount of breadcrumbs. Finish off by sprinkling each fillet with 1 tablespoon of vermouth.

Pour water into the dish around the edges of the fillets to prevent sticking. Place the dish in the oven, and bake for 8 to 10 minutes or until the flesh is opaque and flakes when poked with a fork. Serve immediately with lemon wedge garnish. Serves 4.

Baked Haddock with Caramelized Onion and Bacon

Bayley's Lobster Pound, Scarborough, Maine

¼ pound center-cut bacon, chopped

1 Vidalia onion, chopped

1 tablespoon garlic, chopped

⅔ cup breadcrumbs

1 teaspoon dried thyme

1 tablespoon capers (drained)

1½ pounds fresh haddock fillets

2 tablespoons melted butter

For those who may feel that haddock needs a bit of a flavor boost from time to time, this recipe from Bayley's Lobster Pound in Pine Point, Maine, brings on board some bacon, caramelized onions, and a dash of capers to liven things up.

Preheat oven to 375 degrees. Render the bacon in a sauté pan until crisp, then remove it to drain on a paper towel. Crumble the bacon and set aside.

Add the chopped onion to the bacon fat, and cook over low heat until it's sweet to the taste. Add the garlic, breadcrumbs, thyme, capers, and crumbled bacon to the pan, mix together, then remove the pan from the heat. Coat the haddock fillets in melted butter, and place them in a 9 × 13-inch baking pan. Press the breadcrumb mixture on top of the fillets, and bake in the preheated oven for 15 to 20 minutes, depending on the thickness. The fillets are done when they flake easily at the touch of a fork. Serves 3 to 4.

Tip: All haddock fillets have a thick end and a thin end (head and tail). For even cooking, just fold over a portion of the tail end so that the fillet is an even thickness across in your baking pan.

Bud's Baked Cod or Haddock Fillets

Bud's Fish Market, Branford, Connecticut

2 pounds haddock or codfish fillets

1 tablespoon fresh lemon or lime juice

1 tablespoon mayonnaise

⅛ teaspoon black pepper

½ cup breadcrumbs

2 tablespoons (¼ stick) butter or margarine, melted

2 tablespoons fresh parsley, finely chopped

Preheat the oven to 425 degrees. Place the fish in a baking dish sprayed with cooking oil spray. In a small bowl, combine the lemon or lime juice, mayonnaise, and pepper, and spread the mixture evenly over the fish fillets. Sprinkle the slathered fillets with breadcrumbs and drizzle with butter or margarine.

Bake for 20 minutes or until the fish flakes easily. Adjust the baking time depending on the thickness of the fish. Remove from the oven, sprinkle with fresh parsley, and serve. Serves 4 to 6.

Mediterranean Baked Cod

City Fish Market, Wethersfield, Connecticut

1 cup sweet onion, thinly sliced (Oso Sweet or Vidalia)

2 garlic cloves, minced

2 teaspoons olive oil

12 large fresh basil leaves

2 pounds fresh cod fillet

2 teaspoons salt

2 fresh tomatoes, sliced

¼ cup pitted kalamata olives, sliced

1 medium lemon

½ teaspoon fresh cracked black pepper

Preheat the oven to 425 degrees. In a nonstick skillet, sauté the onions and garlic in the olive oil until tender, then set aside. Coat a 13 × 9-inch baking dish with cooking spray. Arrange the basil leaves in a single layer in the dish, top with the fish fillets, and sprinkle with salt. Top the fillets with the onion mixture from the skillet.

Arrange the tomato slices and kalamata olives over the fillets. Thinly slice half of the lemon and place the slices over the top of the fillets. Squeeze the juice from the remaining lemon half over everything. Top with black pepper.

Cover the baking dish with aluminum foil and bake in the preheated oven for 15 minutes, or until fish flakes easily with a fork. Serves 4 to 6.

Cod Cheeks with White Wine, Lemon, and Garlic Sauce

Nauset Fish and Lobster Pool, Orleans, Massachusetts

1 tablespoon olive oil

3 shallots

2 cloves garlic, minced

1 pound cod cheeks

½ cup white wine

Juice of 1 lemon

¼ teaspoon red chili pepper flakes

¼ cup parsley, finely chopped

Salt and pepper to taste

½ teaspoon flour (if sauce is too thin)

Cod cheeks are quite literally the cheeks of a codfish. These meaty morsels are found around the jaws of large cod, and they're considered quite a delicacy in some circles. If your fish market doesn't carry them, perhaps they can special-order them for you. In olden days, it's said that many cod fishermen would extract the cheeks and throw the rest of the fish away—that's how good these prime pieces of codfish are to people who really know.

Heat the olive oil in a nonstick skillet over medium heat. Add the shallots and sauté until translucent, then add the garlic. Add the cod cheeks and sauté for 2 minutes. Add the wine and lemon juice and cook for 3 minutes or until the cheeks are cooked through. Add the chili pepper flakes and parsley. Add salt and pepper, if desired. Stir in the flour if the sauce is too thin. Serves 2 to 3.

Tip: Sea scallops may be substituted for cod cheeks if they are unavailable.

Baked Haddock with Tomatoes and Capers

Kyler's Catch Seafood Market, New Bedford, Massachusetts

1 cup tomatoes, diced

3 tablespoons olive oil

2 tablespoons capers

1 pound haddock fillets

1 cup panko crumbs

1 teaspoon thyme

Salt and pepper to taste

Preheat the oven to 400 degrees. Mix the tomatoes, olive oil, and capers in a bowl. Place the haddock in a 9 × 13-inch baking dish. Top with the tomatoes, olive oil, and capers mixture.

In another bowl, mix the panko crumbs and thyme. Sprinkle the crumbs and thyme mixture over the fillets and topping. Season with salt and pepper. Bake at 400 degrees for 25 minutes, or until fillets flake easily with a fork.
Serves 2 to 3.

Cape Codder Seafood Market

West Yarmouth, Massachusetts

Many of the seafood markets that used to dot busy and touristy Route 28, between the Cape Cod towns of Falmouth and Chatham, have been made obsolete by grocery store chains that sport their own large seafood departments. One operation that has survived and offers up loads of character and charm (and good seafood) is the Cape Codder Seafood Market in the town of West Yarmouth.

The Cape Codder resides on the south side of Route 28, in a weathered, cedar-shingled, Cape-style house that's a throwback to a different era. With all the nautical kitsch nailed to the exterior and the FISH MKT sign affixed to the roof, it's

clear that it's been a while since the building has served as a family home. In fact, it's been a few different fish markets over the past several decades. At one point, a hurricane storm surge lifted and pushed the building across to the north side of Route 28, then gingerly moved it back. The market is actually part of a complex that includes the adjacent Lobster Boat restaurant, which sports an actual fishing boat–cum–bar permanently sunk into the restaurant's front yard.

Mark VanBuskirk is the current owner of the Cape Codder, which he took over in 2007. It's a straightforward seafood market, featuring fresh fish fillets, shellfish, and prepared foods like stuffed scallops and boiled shrimp in two display cases in the center of the store. (One item of note is the Nantucket bay scallops, an excellent choice when they're in season.)

The market's seafood cases are flanked by shelves of condiments and specialty items on one side, and by a large lobster tank on the other. Mark has a culinary background, and for a number of years he served as the cook on a National Oceanic and Atmospheric Administration research vessel. He likes to cook up prepared meals, and he stocks his refrigerated cases full of them in the front of the store.

Mark's customers love coming here, and they don't want him to change a thing about the place. He says it reminds them of how Cape Cod used to be—more homey, more personable, more friendly—and that's fine with him. Here's hoping the Cape Codder can keep on in its idiosyncratic way for many years to come.

Haddock au Gratin

Cape Codder Seafood Market, West Yarmouth, Massachusetts

AU GRATIN SAUCE

1 tablespoon butter

2 tablespoons onion, chopped

3 cups light cream

Pinch of salt

Cornstarch slurry (follow
    instructions on the box)

2 cups light yellow shredded
    cheddar cheese

1 tablespoon cooking sherry

CRUMB COATING

¼ cup (½ stick) butter

1 sleeve Ritz crackers, crumbled
    finely

1 pound haddock (cod or any other
    white fish may be substituted)

Lemon juice (optional)

This old-time seafood market on Route 28 in the heart of touristy Cape Cod has weathered lots of ups and downs. One of the consistently favorite dishes they've made over the years in their prepared foods section is this belly-warming rendition of baked haddock, with a rich, creamy, crunchy au gratin coating.

To make the au gratin sauce, melt the butter in a saucepan, and sauté the onion in the butter over medium heat. Add the cream and salt, bring the mixture to steaming without boiling, and slowly stir in the cornstarch slurry until the sauce thickens. Turn off the heat and add the cheese and sherry, stirring constantly until thoroughly mixed and thickened. (It's good to make the sauce thick, as the fish will release its juices while it cooks, giving the sauce a nice consistency.)

To make the crumb coating, melt the stick of butter in another saucepan, and mix in the Ritz crumbs. Set aside, or do this ahead of time. Keep any extra buttered crumbs in the freezer for another time.

Preheat the oven to 375 degrees. Pour and spread half the cheese sauce into a baking pan, and place the fillets on top of the layer of sauce. Spread the rest of the cheese sauce over the fish fillets, and top it with the buttered crumb mix. You may wish to squeeze some lemon juice on top before baking.

Bake in the oven for about 15 minutes, until the fillets are golden brown on top.

Variation: Add scallops, shrimp, and/or lobster meat to make the dish a seafood au gratin.

Cod alla Puttanesca

R&D Seafood, Woonsocket, Rhode Island

1 tablespoon olive oil

1 small onion, chopped

2 garlic cloves, minced

1 15-ounce can diced tomatoes

1 small can (2¼ ounces) sliced black olives, drained

1 tablespoon capers

1 teaspoon dried oregano leaves

1¼ pounds cod fillets

1 tablespoon parsley, chopped

Preheat the oven to 375 degrees. Heat the olive oil in a large frying pan over medium-high heat. Add the onion and cook, stirring, until golden, about 3 to 4 minutes. Add the garlic and stir until fragrant, about 1 minute. Add the tomatoes and their juice, olives, capers, and oregano. Boil uncovered until most of the liquid cooks away, about 6 to 8 minutes.

Lightly oil a baking dish that will hold the fillets in a single layer. Arrange the fish in the dish, tucking thin tail sections under. Pour the sauce over the cod, and bake until the fish is just opaque in the center, about 15 to 20 minutes. Remove from the oven, sprinkle with parsley, and serve. Serves 3.

R&D Seafood

Woonsocket, Rhode Island

"R&D" stands for Raymond and Doris (Charest), who founded this Blackstone Valley seafood market in Woonsocket in 1968. Today, the seafood retailer and wholesaler is run by the Charests' sons, Ronald and Mark, who purchased the business from their parents in 1990. Worry not that this establishment is somewhat distant from the ocean's shores: R&D makes daily runs to the fish piers in New Bedford and Boston in order to keep their store stocked with some of the finest fish and shellfish to be found in southern New England.

R&D is housed in a brick-and-wood building next to Barry Field, not far from the heart of town. The market's white-on-white interior bespeaks the cleanliness of the place, and the hard-working Charest brothers keep it that way at all times. They've got a friendly staff who are well-versed in all things seafood and who are ready to answer any questions or fill any needs that you may have.

All the standard New England seafood that you would expect to find closer to the shoreline may be found here. The filleted fish are hand-cut on the premises for ultimate freshness. You may choose from such stalwarts as fresh cod, haddock, swordfish, Canadian salmon, and flounder, as well as more exotic fare, such as Chilean sea bass and wild-caught Alaskan sockeye salmon. Shellfish standouts include sea and bay scallops, chopped sea clams, chopped quahogs, Maine steamers, Prince Edward Island mussels, and live lobsters in an array of sizes.

Prepared foods include stuffed quahogs ("stuffies"), shrimp or lobster egg rolls, various chowders, shrimp or lobster bisque, and oven-ready scallops or scrod. Be sure to pick up a bag of Drum Rock Fritter and Clam Cake Mix or its competitor, Krisppe Famous Rhode Island Clam Cake Mix, both of local origin and essential ingredients when making classic Rhode Island clam fritters at home.

Spanish-Style Roasted Cod and Littleneck Clams on Potato Slices

R&D Seafood, Woonsocket, Rhode Island

4 teaspoons olive oil, divided

1 pound potatoes, preferably Yukon gold, peeled and thinly sliced

Salt and freshly ground pepper, to taste

2 teaspoons fresh thyme, chopped and divided

1 pound fresh cod or haddock fillets

Pinch of red pepper flakes (optional)

1 tablespoon breadcrumbs

1 tablespoon unsalted butter, cut into small cubes

18 littleneck clams, scrubbed clean

3 tablespoons fresh parsley, chopped (optional)

Roasting cod and clams together in the oven is a year-round treat that's simple to prepare and relatively easy on the pocketbook. The thin-sliced potatoes round out this dish very nicely.

Position a rack in the middle of the oven and preheat the oven to 400 degrees. Grease the bottom of a large (about 14-inch) gratin dish, ovenproof skillet, or earthenware dish with 1 teaspoon of the olive oil. Arrange the potato slices in an overlapping pattern to create one layer. Season liberally with the salt and pepper and 1 teaspoon of the thyme. Brush the top with 2 teaspoons of the olive oil, and bake for 20 minutes.

Remove the potatoes from the oven, and raise the temperature to 450 degrees. Place the cod fillets on top of the potatoes, and brush with the remaining teaspoon of olive oil. Season with salt and pepper, the remaining teaspoon of thyme, and the red pepper flakes, if desired. Sprinkle with the breadcrumbs and top with the butter cubes. Place the clams around the cod, next to the rims of the baking dish. Bake for 10 minutes.

Remove from the oven and carefully flip the clams over, to release their juices, without disturbing any of the potatoes. Roast for another 5 to 8 minutes, or until the clams have just opened and the fish is opaque. Remove from the oven, baste the top of the fish with the clam juices, and serve immediately, sprinkled with the parsley. Serves 3 to 4.

Panko-Crusted Haddock with Spicy Herb Mayo

New Deal Fish Market, Cambridge, Massachusetts

SPICY HERB MAYO

¼ cup mayonnaise

½ teaspoon sriracha chili sauce

½ tablespoon honey

Large pinch tarragon, chopped

1 squeeze of lemon juice

2 haddock fillets (4–6 ounces each), skinned (your seafood market can do this)

1 egg, beaten

1 cup panko

¼ cup canola or mild olive oil

Combine all the ingredients for the Spicy Herb Mayo in a bowl, and mix thoroughly. Set aside.

Dip the haddock fillets in the beaten egg and dredge on a plate covered in panko. Fry in canola or mild olive oil on medium to high heat, turning once, until lightly browned. Drizzle the spicy herb mayo on top or on the side of your plate. Serves 2.

Tip: You may substitute any fresh white fish fillet for haddock.

Blount Market

Warren, Rhode Island

Eastern Rhode Island is full of surprises—towns with pretty, quaint houses, lots of little bays and inlets off of Narragansett Bay, and Main Streets that take you back to a simpler, quieter time. In the midst of this setting, in beautiful Warren, Rhode Island, you'll find the Blount Market, a retail offshoot of the nearby Blount Fine Foods seaside production facility that makes gourmet chowder for some of the finest restaurants and shops in the country.

The Blount family started their shellfish business as an oyster operation in the 1880s. The hurricane of 1938 wiped out the nearby oyster beds in Narragansett Bay, so the family turned its attention to clams and, by extension, chowders. Though they have sold their clams in bulk to the likes of Campbell's, Panera Bread, and Legal Sea Foods, they've recently developed a nice core business of high-end soups, sauces, side dishes, and entrees, and they sell many of them through the quaint, one-room Blount Market on Water Street.

The Blount Market grew out of another seafood retailer, Hall's Seafood, which was established in 1978. Tom and Emily Hall opened their shop in Warren and sold the fish and shellfish that they caught daily using their family's fishing boat. A friendly business relationship developed between the Halls and the Blounts, and in 2005 Todd Blount made an offer and acquired the retail business from the Halls, renaming it Blount Market.

This charming retail spot resides in a small, beige building with a green awning over the front door that beckons visitors to enter and behold the treasures within. The pine board and ceramic tile interior is warm and inviting, and the shelves and refrigerated cases are bursting with fresh and prepared foods of all sorts.

First and foremost here are the famous chowders and bisques that Blount is known for. In addition to the excellent lobster bisques and clam chowders (white and red), there are such specialties as scallop and bacon chowder and shrimp and corn chowder. Most come in perfectly sealed plastic bags that you immerse in boiling water for 40 minutes or so, then cut open and enjoy. Other soup and chowder standouts include Portuguese kale soup, spiced pumpkin bisque, Tuscan bean and sausage soup, potato, roasted garlic, and leek soup, and several different types of chili.

The two seafood cases at the center of the store are chock-full of fresh, often locally caught finned fish and shellfish (Blount has its own scallop and lobster boats). They also sell an array of prepared foods, such as lobster mac and cheese, various types of seafood cakes, and exotic salads like their quinoa and rice salad with kale, mango, feta, dried cranberries, and almonds.

There's a lobster tank on the premises, if you wish to procure some "bugs" to take home and cook up. Be sure not to miss the refrigerated case full of various types of "stuffies" and dinners like scallops wrapped in bacon. And perhaps the best part of the whole operation is the Bargain Corner, where you'll fine large, frozen bags of chowder and other goodies from Blount's overstock at more than reasonable prices.

As if all this isn't enough, Blount owns a delightful clam shack housed in a couple of royal blue trailers down by the waterfront across the street. Here you may partake of Blount's famous clam chowder and order up a basket of perfectly fried clams. The market and shack are quite a one-two punch that will knock you out and win you over for the good life in eastern Rhode Island.

Scrod Gratin

Blount Market, Warren, Rhode Island

2 cups Panera Bread Broccoli and Cheddar Soup (or similar broccoli and cheddar soup)

2 cups broccoli florets, lightly steamed

1 pound scrod fillets

½ cup shredded cheddar cheese

½ cup shredded Monterey Jack cheese

½ cup green onions, finely minced

Scrod is a young codfish, but you may use any whitefish for this simple recipe that's equal parts healthy and cheesy.

Preheat the oven to 375 degrees. Lightly spray a medium-size casserole dish with nonstick cooking spray, or lightly coat with vegetable oil.

Pour ½ cup of soup on the bottom of the dish, and arrange the lightly steamed broccoli in a single layer on the bottom. Lay the scrod fillets over the broccoli, and pour the remaining soup over the top.

Sprinkle the shredded cheddar and Monterey Jack cheeses over the top. Bake until golden, about 22 to 25 minutes. Remove from oven and sprinkle green onions over the top before serving. Serves 3 to 4.

Codfish Provençale

Champlin's Seafood, Narragansett, Rhode Island

1 pound codfish fillets

1 tomato, thinly sliced

2 thin slices red onion or sweet
   onion

½ teaspoon garlic powder

¼ cup (½ stick) butter, melted

1 ounce white wine

1 tablespoon lemon juice

½ cup flavored breadcrumbs
   (optional)

Preheat the oven to 350 degrees. Lay the codfish in a baking pan, then place the sliced tomato and onion on top of the codfish.

Mix the garlic powder with the melted butter, and pour on top of the fish, along with the white wine and lemon juice. Top the fillets with a sprinkling of breadcrumbs, if desired.

Bake in the preheated oven for half an hour or until the cod fillets begin to flake. Serve with your favorite steamed vegetable or salad and rice of any sort on the side. Serves 2 to 3.

Slim, Italian-Style "Fried" Scrod

R&D Seafood, Woonsocket, Rhode Island

1 pound fresh haddock, cod, or
   pollock

½ cup Italian dressing

½ cup unseasoned breadcrumbs

The only thing Italian about this recipe is the salad dressing marinade. The beauty of it, however, is in the simplicity—quick, fresh fish "fried" up in no time.

Preheat the oven to 450 degrees. Divide the fish into two pieces. Marinate the fish portions in the dressing in a shallow bowl for 15 minutes, turning frequently.

Spray a cookie sheet with nonstick cooking spray. Sprinkle the breadcrumbs on a shallow plate. Press each marinated fish portion in the breadcrumbs, coating both sides lightly. Arrange the pieces in a single layer on the cookie sheet. Bake in the preheated oven for 6 to 8 minutes per side, turning once. Serves 2.

FLOUNDER AND SOLE

Richie's Quick Sole

Wulf's Fish Market, Brookline, Massachusetts

1 pound grey sole fillets

1 cup light cream or half-and-half

2 cups seasoned breadcrumbs

3–4 tablespoons olive or other
    cooking oil, divided

Richie Taylor, of Wulf's Fish Market in Brookline, Massachusetts, recommends this no-nonsense way to bake up a quick fish dinner.

Preheat the oven to 350 degrees. In a shallow dish, wet the sole with the cream. In another shallow dish, coat each fillet with the breadcrumbs.

Lightly oil a baking sheet, and place the fillets on it, leaving space between each one. Lightly baste the fillets with the rest of the cooking oil. Bake at 350 degrees for 20 minutes. Serve immediately. Serves 2 to 3.

Parmesan-Herb Baked Flounder

City Fish Market, Wethersfield, Connecticut

4 6-ounce flounder fillets

⅓ cup grated Parmesan cheese

¼ cup low-fat mayonnaise

2 tablespoons green onions, minced

¼ cup dry breadcrumbs

1 teaspoon dried basil

1 teaspoon dried oregano

¼ teaspoon salt

¼ teaspoon pepper

Flounder is a thin, light fish fillet with mild flavor that should be watched carefully while it's in the oven to avoid overcooking. Your diligence will be rewarded with a nicely seasoned fish dish that even avowed seafood-haters at your table will enjoy.

Preheat the oven to 400 degrees. Lay the fillets out on a foil-lined baking sheet that has been coated with cooking spray. In a bowl, mix together the cheese, mayonnaise, and onions; spread the mixture evenly over the fish.

Mix together the breadcrumbs and the remaining ingredients; sprinkle evenly over the fish. Lightly coat the fish with a spritz of the cooking spray. Bake for 10 minutes or until the fish flakes easily. Remove carefully with a spatula from the baking sheet and foil. Serves 4.

Seasonal Sole Piccata

Nauset Fish and Lobster Pool, Orleans, Massachusetts

2 tablespoons olive oil

1 pound sole (or flounder) fillets
(approximately 4 pieces)

Salt and pepper to taste

¼ cup flour

¼ cup white wine

Juice of 2 lemons

2 tablespoons capers

2 tablespoons butter

This is an excellent wintertime seafood dish that's easily prepared on the stovetop. It's light, flaky, and pairs well with fresh steamed vegetables, salad, or a pasta or rice pilaf.

Heat the olive oil in a sauté pan over medium-high heat. Season the fish with salt and pepper. Dredge the fillets in the flour, shaking off the excess.

Sauté the fillets in the pan for 4 minutes, flipping them halfway through. Remove the fillets and set aside.

Deglaze the pan with the wine, and whisk for 1 minute. Add the lemon juice and capers, and stir. Whisk in the butter until well blended. Pour the sauce over the fillets and serve. Serves 2 to 3.

Flanders' Flounder Florentine

Flanders Fish Market, East Lyme, Connecticut

4 6-ounce flounder fillets, rinsed and patted dry with a paper towel (put in refrigerator if not using immediately)

Coarse salt and fresh-ground black pepper

1 cup all-purpose flour

½ cup olive oil

½ cup leeks, white part only, rinsed thoroughly and diced

¼ cup sherry

2 teaspoons garlic, minced

2 tablespoons butter, melted

4 cups fresh baby spinach leaves, rinsed and dried

1 lemon, cut into wedges

This spinach-enhanced flounder recipe from Flanders Fish Market is as healthy as it is flavorful.

Season the flounder fillets lightly with salt and pepper. Dredge the fillets in the flour, and shake off any excess. Set aside.

In a sauté pan, heat the olive oil over medium heat. Toss the leeks in the olive oil and sauté for 1 to 2 minutes. Place the flounder in the pan, and allow it to cook for about 5 minutes. Flip the fillets, add the sherry, and cover the pan. Cook for 3 to 4 minutes longer, then remove the pan from the heat and set aside.

In another sauté pan over medium heat, sauté the garlic in the butter for about 1 minute. Add the spinach to the pan, and season lightly with salt and pepper. Sauté the spinach for about 2 minutes, then cover and set aside. The spinach will finish cooking on its own.

Place the spinach on a warm plate and top with the fillets. Serve with a lemon wedge garnish. Serves 4.

Bud's Baked Stuffed Lemon Sole

Bud's Fish Market, Branford, Connecticut

STUFFING

½ pound lump crabmeat

½ pound scallops, chopped

½ pound raw shrimp, peeled, deveined, and chopped

1 package seafood stuffing mix

Splash of sherry

4 tablespoons (½ stick) butter, melted

Salt and pepper to taste

2 pounds (8–10) sole fillets, thin enough for rolling

Butter pats or olive oil

Paprika (optional)

Lemon wedges

This rich yet healthy dish goes well with steamed asparagus and a rice pilaf on the side. The stuffing is chock-full of seafood goodness. Be sure to ask for thin fillets at the seafood market, so you can roll them up with the stuffing inside.

Preheat the oven to 375 degrees. Mix all the stuffing ingredients together to form a sticky substance that holds together like dough.

Lay each fillet flat on a clean counter or cutting board. Place about 2 heaping tablespoons of the seafood stuffing mixture in the middle of each fillet, and roll each one up like a jellyroll.

Top each roll with a small pat of butter or few drops of olive oil. Sprinkle with a little paprika, if desired. Spray cooking oil in the baking pan, and place the rolled fillets about 1 to 2 inches apart. (You may need more than one baking pan.)

Bake for 20 minutes. Serves 8 to 10.

Pan-Fried Flounder

City Fish Market, Wethersfield, Connecticut

4 flounder fillets (skinless)

Salt and pepper to taste

Flour, for dredging fish

2 tablespoons vegetable oil

3 tablespoons butter, divided

Juice of 1 lemon

1 small bottle capers

Wash the fillets in cold water and pat dry. Sprinkle each with salt and pepper, and then dredge the fillets in flour.

Place the vegetable oil and 2 tablespoons of butter in a flat, heavy-bottomed skillet, and heat on medium-high until the butter melts. Keeping heat at medium-high, cook the fish on one side for about 3 minutes (more or less, depending on size of fillets), until it's deep brown and crispy. Turn the fish carefully, and cook on the other side for about 2 to 3 minutes. Turn the fish only once. Remove the fish to a serving platter.

Turn off the stove heat. Into the still-hot skillet, whisk in the remaining tablespoon of butter. Add the lemon juice, then pour in the capers, liquid and all. Continue to whisk until you have a thin sauce.

Pour the sauce over the fish fillets, and serve at once. Serves 4.

Friday Fish Fry

David's Fish Market and Lobster Pound, Salisbury, Massachusetts

½ cup olive oil

2 eggs

½ cup milk

1 pound flounder or sole fillets

2 cups Italian-style breadcrumbs

Fried fish on Fridays has been a staple for American Catholics everywhere, and it's become a welcome tradition among the American mainstream—especially in New England, where thin, flaky, fresh fish fillets abound in seafood markets and sell rapidly with the weekend approaching.

Pour and heat the olive oil in a large skillet over medium heat.

Mix the egg and milk in a shallow bowl to make a wash. Pour the breadcrumbs into a shallow dish or plate. Dip the fish into the egg-and-milk wash, let the excess drip off, then coat both sides of each fillet with breadcrumbs. Repeat the process with each fillet for a nice coating.

Carefully place the breaded fish into the hot oil, and cook about 2 minutes on each side. Serves 2 to 3.

Options: Add grated Parmesan cheese, garlic powder, or both to your breadcrumbs before coating the fillets to boost the flavor.

Flounder with Shiitake Mushrooms in Fresh Tomato Sauce

R&D Seafood, Woonsocket, Rhode Island

2 tablespoons olive oil

½ pound shiitake mushrooms, stemmed

1 garlic clove, minced and thinly sliced

½ cup dry white wine

2 medium tomatoes, peeled, seeded, and chopped

½ teaspoon salt

¼ teaspoon pepper

4 flounder fillets, 6 ounces each

Preheat oven to 450 degrees. In a large skillet, heat the olive oil over medium-high heat. Add the mushrooms and garlic. Cook, tossing occasionally, until the mushrooms are slightly wilted and lightly browned, about 3 minutes. Pour in the wine, increase the heat to high, and boil until reduced by half. Add the tomatoes, salt, and pepper. Bring to a boil and cook, stirring occasionally, until slightly thickened, about 3 minutes.

Arrange the flounder fillets in a baking dish large enough to hold them flat. Pour the mushrooms and sauce over the fish. Cover the baking dish tightly with aluminum foil and bake 10 minutes, or until the fish is firm and opaque throughout. Serves 4.

Superior Lemon Sole Piccata

Superior Seafood, Westport, Connecticut

½ cup flour

Salt

Pepper

Garlic powder

1 pound sole fillets

¼ cup olive oil

2 tablespoons margarine

½ cup white wine

1 cup chicken broth

Juice of 1 lemon

Parsley

The piccata method of cooking usually applies to skinless, boneless chicken breasts or veal, pounded flat and flavored with lemon, wine, and chicken broth, but it also works very nicely with thin, tender fillets of sole (minus the pounding, of course).

Mix the flour, salt, pepper, and garlic powder, and dredge the fish fillets with the mixture on a plate or other flat surface. Sauté the fish in a frying pan with the oil and margarine, over medium heat, until the fillets are lightly browned on both sides. Place the fish on paper towels to drain.

Add the white wine to the frying pan, turn up the heat, and cook until the wine has reduced by half. Add the chicken broth, lemon juice, and parsley. Put the fish back into the pan and simmer for 15 minutes. Serve the fillets with thin slices of lemon on top. Serves 2.

SHRIMP

David and Manuela's Asian Shrimp

David's Fish Market, Fall River, Massachusetts

MARINADE

½ cup coconut milk

5 tablespoons fish sauce

¼ cup light brown sugar

2 tablespoons soy sauce

Juice of 2 fresh limes

2 tablespoons Stop & Shop Five-Spice Powder

1 teaspoon crushed red pepper flakes

1 tablespoon curry powder

4 garlic cloves, chopped

2 pounds raw shrimp, peeled and deveined (13–15 or 16–20 per pound)

Vietnamese dipping sauce

This is Manuela Sardinha's favorite dish to prepare at home when she's not working at David's Fish Market, in the Portuguese section of Fall River, Massachusetts. It brings together a vast range of spices blended into a coconut milk marinade.

Place all the ingredients for the marinade in a blender and purée. Pour the marinade over the shrimp in a sealable container, and marinate for at least four hours in the refrigerator or 1½ hours at room temperature.

Preheat the grill. Remove the shrimp from the container and discard the marinade. Grill the shrimp, turning frequently, until just cooked through. Serve with Vietnamese dipping sauce. Serves 8 to 10 as an appetizer or 5 to 6 as a main course.

Bud's Baked Stuffed Shrimp

Bud's Fish Market, Branford, Connecticut

STUFFING

1 bag or box seafood stuffing mix

½ pound lump crabmeat

⅓ pound sea scallops, chopped

¼ teaspoon garlic salt

⅛ teaspoon pepper

2 tablespoons fresh parsley, chopped

½ cup melted butter

¼ cup sherry wine

8 under-8-count jumbo raw shrimp, shells on

Dash of paprika (if desired)

This recipe calls for super jumbo shrimp, which work best and make for an excellent presentation. If you can't find under-8-count shrimp, go with the biggest ones you can get.

Preheat the oven to 425 degrees. Mix all the ingredients for the stuffing until it achieves a sticky consistency and holds together well.

Butterfly the shrimp. With clean hands, carefully stuff each shrimp with the stuffing, and place them in a baking dish that is coated with a little cooking oil or spray. Sprinkle with a bit of paprika, if desired.

Bake for 20 minutes, remove from the oven, and serve. Serves 4 to 6.

Port Lobster Company

Kennebunkport, Maine

As you travel the mile or so along the river from Kennebunk-port's central business district, toward the ocean and George H. W. Bush's stately home on Walker's Point, you pass by a small, pretty brick building on the left with a wooden PORT LOBSTER sign nailed to the wall. This unprepossessing place is home to one of the oldest and largest lobster distributors in the area—as well as a first-class fish market with a lot more than just lobster within.

Port Lobster dates its founding back to 1953, when Sonny Hutchins and a partner opened a lobster distribution business in Kennebunkport, at that time a sleepy little seaside town with a modest summertime tourist trade. The partner bowed out of the business later that first year, and Sonny and his family have been the owners ever since. Sonny's father was a lobsterman in the area for 44 years and lived to be 100 years and one week old before passing on, so lobster fishing is tightly woven into the family's fabric. At one time, as many as 22 lobster boats fished exclusively for Port Lobster. That number has dropped to eight in recent years, but those boats still supply more than enough lobsters to keep the business going strong.

Some time around the turn of the millennium, Port Lobster expanded its modest retail lobster business into other types of seafood, prepared foods, and baked goods, all aimed at the locals and the summer crowds that have mobbed the area ever since the elder Bush captured the White House in 1988. Sonny's daughter Kathy Anuszewski has been handling day-to-day operations of the fish market for quite a while, running it efficiently and effectively for the regular customers and the tourists alike.

Port Lobster prides itself in buying nearly all its fish and lobster from local fishermen, many of them day boaters in the immediate vicinity. Though lobster is still what they're best known for, they keep their seafood case stocked with cod, haddock, swordfish, halibut, flounder, grey sole, hake, scallops, clams, oysters, mussels, and shrimp at all times. Their delivery bay is right next to the front door, so don't be surprised if you see a fisherman dropping off a day's catch while you're there.

There are all sorts of interesting prepared foods for folks to take home and heat up for lunch or dinner. Some of the regularly featured items include lobster mac and cheese (including a gluten-free version), lobster bisque, lobster Newburg, seafood casseroles, shrimp and pasta salads, lobster corn fritters, crab-stuffed deviled eggs, and individual-size lobster and artichoke "pizzas" made using pita bread. There's also a short menu of carry-out sandwiches with a very affordable lobster roll leading the way. For a couple of bucks extra, you may upgrade it to a lunch box, which comes with coleslaw and a bag of chips. The homemade chowders are also excellent.

The icing on the cake here is the impressive variety of baked goods that Kathy and her crew produce in the back kitchen every day—items like cheddar cheese biscuits, strawberry rhubarb crisp, baguettes, cookies, Maine rhubarb crisp, cream biscuits, and more. Rare is the fish market that does so much baking, especially given the market's diminutive size.

Port Lobster is a great place to get off the beaten path a bit in Kennebunkport. Sit in one of the Adirondack chairs out front, enjoy a freshly made lobster roll, then procure some fresh seafood to cook up for dinner that night. Just follow the Kennebunk River to where it meets the ocean.

Port Lobster Oven-Roasted Shrimp

Port Lobster Company, Kennebunkport, Maine

2 pounds (16 to 20 per pound) raw
    shrimp, peeled and deveined,
    with tail on

1–2 tablespoons olive oil

Salt and pepper to taste

This recipe calls for jumbo shrimp, which are generally the best shrimp to serve on their own as an appetizer or main course and not as part of a rice- or pasta-based dish. Larger shrimp are meatier and more rich and dense in flavor, making them well worth the extra per-pound price you usually pay to procure them.

Preheat the oven to 425 degrees. Place the shrimp in a large bowl and drizzle with the olive oil, salt, and pepper. Place the shrimp on a parchment-lined baking sheet, spreading them out in one layer.

Roast the shrimp for 10 to 15 minutes. Using tongs, turn each shrimp over and roast until the shrimp are opaque in color. Serve as an appetizer with cocktail sauce or as a meal with rice pilaf and a green salad on the side. Serves 12 as an appetizer or 6 as a meal.

Dad's Famous Stuffed Shrimp

R&D Seafood, Woonsocket, Rhode Island

12 jumbo (16–20 count) shrimp

4 ounces bay scallops (chopped sea scallops may be substituted)

4 tablespoons butter, divided

½ cup water

4 ounces crabmeat

½ cup Ritz crackers, crushed

½ cup Saltine crackers, crushed

Preheat the oven to 375 degrees. Peel and devein the shrimp, leaving the tails intact. Remove and discard the large vein running along the back of the shrimp. Cut the scallops into small pieces.

In a small saucepan, combine the scallops, 2 tablespoons butter, and the water. Boil the scallops until cooked through, about one minute. Drain the scallops, reserving the liquid.

Shred the crabmeat, and melt the remaining 2 tablespoons of butter in the pan. Combine the crabmeat, scallops, Ritz crackers, Saltines, and melted butter. Mix well. Add in the reserved liquid in small amounts, until the stuffing reaches the desired consistency.

Split the shrimp along the back, and arrange on a greased cookie sheet. Place an equal amount of the stuffing on each of the shrimp. Sprinkle with paprika, if desired. Bake 20 minutes or until cooked through. Serves 4.

Shrimp or Scallops, Scampi Style

Superior Seafood, Westport, Connecticut

2 teaspoons garlic, chopped

¼ cup olive oil

½ cup white wine

Salt

Pepper

1½–2 pounds shrimp or scallops

Fresh parsley

Breadcrumbs

Parmesan cheese

Paprika

Scampi is an Italian word meaning "prawn," or large shrimp. In many Italian-American restaurants, you'll find Shrimp Scampi, which actually describes the cooking method, calling for garlic, butter, breadcrumbs, and often Parmesan cheese. This scampi recipe works with either shrimp or scallops. (If you use sea scallops, you may wish to halve or quarter them before cooking, depending on their size.)

In a large oven-proof skillet over medium-high heat, sauté the garlic in the olive oil. Add the wine and salt and pepper to taste, then let the mixture reduce by half, about 5 minutes. After the garlic turns light brown, add the shrimp or scallops to the pan. Cook the scallops on both sides until the tops of the scallops are cracked, or cook the shrimp until they're pink or curled, then add the parsley and breadcrumbs on top. Sprinkle on some Parmesan cheese and paprika. Place under the broiler for a few minutes until golden brown (watch carefully to avoid drying out), then serve immediately. Serves 4 to 6.

Cilantro Lime Shrimp

Flanders Fish Market, East Lyme, Connecticut

1 pound large (26/30 count) raw shrimp, peeled, tails removed, and deveined

2 tablespoons blackened seasoning

2 tablespoons garlic, minced

¼ cup olive oil

¾ cup sherry (not cooking sherry)

Juice of 3 limes

1 cup cilantro, leaves only, roughly chopped

Coarse salt and freshly ground black pepper, to taste

This is a simple and refreshing way to serve shrimp in the summertime. You can serve it over lightly dressed greens or atop fresh-cooked pasta or rice.

In a small bowl, toss the shrimp in the blackened seasoning, turning to coat evenly (the more seasoning you use, the hotter the dish will be). Set the bowl aside.

In a large sauté pan over medium heat, sauté the garlic in olive oil for 1 to 2 minutes. Pour in the sherry and allow the alcohol to burn off. If your pan is hot enough, the alcohol may ignite, so be careful. The flame will only last a few seconds until the alcohol has burned off.

Add the shrimp to the pan and sauté for 5 to 6 minutes. Turn over and cook an additional 3 to 4 minutes. Be careful not to overcook the shrimp—they are cooked through when they become white and lose their opaque coloring.

Turn off the heat. Stir in the lime juice and cilantro. Season to taste with salt and pepper. Serve immediately. Serves 2 to 3.

Donahue's Fish Market

Plaistow, New Hampshire

Not all top-shelf fish markets are hard by the sea. Take, for example, Donahue's Fish Market, in the southern New Hampshire town of Plaistow, just over the border from the Boston metro area. It lies approximately 40 miles north of the city and 15 miles due west of Salisbury, Massachusetts, on a busy commercial stretch of highway.

This somewhat hidden retail market is tucked into a below-street-level space in a split-level building that also houses a tavern. After entering through the front door, you descend a few steps before reaching the compact, well-laid-out seafood market and shack stand.

The Donahue family's history in the seafood business stretches back to 1970, when Charles Donahue began selling fresh seafood from the back of his truck. Soon thereafter, he rented a store in Derry, New Hampshire, and plied his trade for five years before moving the business and the family home down the road to Plaistow.

In 1985, Charles and his wife, Dotty, opened two additional seafood businesses in Rockland and St. George, Maine, leaving their Plaistow store in the capable hands of their children, who had worked there since high school. After Charles passed away, in 1993, the family sold the Maine businesses and Dotty returned to Plaistow to be closer to her family.

Today, Donahue's is run by two of Dottie's children, Mark and Jennifer. They've done a marvelous job of keeping their fish market thriving while simultaneously adding a meat market and deli and a seafood takeout business. They've built a loyal local following over the years, and even pull in some traffic off nearby I-495 during the busy tourist season.

What makes this place special is the hands-on approach of the brother-and-sister team. Mark hand-cuts virtually all the fish found in the seafood case, and Jennifer is ever-present,

Jennifer Marois

attending to a multitude of details that keep the place running smoothly at all times. The best seafood markets tend to be the ones that are family-owned, where the family members are on hand at all times, and Donahue's is one of them.

Much of the seafood offerings come from the ports of Gloucester and New Bedford, with regular deliveries from both. Among the more unusual and intriguing offerings in the prepared foods section are fisherman's pie, lobster mac and cheese, large stuffed clams, and salmon burgers with spinach and feta cheese. The clam and oyster offerings are as good and plentiful as you'll find anywhere, and the plump sea scallops from New Bedford are available nearly year-round.

There are seven lobster tanks on the premises, capable of holding lobsters from chicken size (1-pound) to big boys north of 10 pounds. Donahue's will be happy to cook up your lobster for you, saving you the hassle and mess of doing it at home. There's also a constant supply of fresh-picked lobster meat in the seafood case that's very competitively priced.

Last but not least, the busy kitchen here serves up some great deep-fried seafood, including haddock, whole-belly and strip clams, and various seafood combination platters. There are also a couple of grilled seafood plates (salmon and swordfish) as well as several healthy garden salads, most of them tricked out with seafood, chicken, or steak.

Shrimp with Crabmeat Stuffing

Donahue's Fish Market, Plaistow, New Hampshire

CRABMEAT STUFFING

¼ cup (½ stick) butter

2 teaspoons garlic, minced

2 stalks celery, minced

¼ pound crabmeat

2 tablespoons lemon juice

1 sleeve Ritz crackers, crushed

¼ cup parsley, chopped fine

2 tablespoons Parmesan cheese, grated

12 jumbo shrimp (16–20 count or 21–25 count), peeled, deveined, and butterflied (split lengthwise so that they lie open with a hinge along one side)

Preheat the oven to 350 degrees. Melt the butter in a medium-size saucepan, add the minced garlic and celery, and sauté until soft. Add the crabmeat and lemon juice, then cook for 1 minute, stirring lightly.

In a bowl, combine the Ritz crackers, parsley, and grated Parmesan cheese. Fold in all the ingredients from the saucepan. The mixture should be moist enough to stick together and mold when pinched. Stuff each shrimp with some stuffing, and bake in the preheated oven for 10 to 12 minutes. Serves 6 to 8 for appetizers, or 3 to 4 for dinner.

Gambas al Ajillo

Wulf's Fish Market, Brookline, Massachusetts

1 pound raw jumbo shrimp, peeled and deveined

Salt to taste

5 tablespoons olive oil

6 cloves garlic, peeled and sliced

½ tablespoon red pepper flakes

Juice of ½ lemon

1 tablespoon white wine

A few flat-leaf parsley sprigs

This tongue twister translates from Spanish into "garlic shrimp." How irresistible is that? This very simple dish makes a great appetizer but may also be pumped up to entrée status by increasing the quantities of each ingredient.

Sprinkle the peeled and deveined shrimp with salt.

Heat the oil, garlic, and red pepper flakes in a skillet over medium-high heat. Once the garlic begins to brown, add the shrimp and cook until just done (pink). Add in the lemon juice, white wine, and parsley, and serve immediately. Serves 5 to 6 for an appetizer.

David's Mozambique-Style Shrimp

David's Fish Market, Fall River, Massachusetts

4 tablespoons olive oil

2 pounds (21–25 or 26–30 count) raw shrimp, shell-on, or shelled and deveined

4 tablespoons garlic powder

2 tablespoons butter

½ cup white wine

Juice of 1 lemon

½ cup milk (optional)

1–2 tablespoons Frank's Red Hot Sauce (or other hot sauce)

Mozambique was once a colony of Portugal, and this recipe made its way to David's Fish Market in Fall River through its Portuguese ancestry. Its sauce is an unusual mixture of wine and milk, flavored with garlic, butter, lemon, and a healthy dose of hot sauce.

Heat the olive oil in a large, deep frying pan over medium heat, then sauté the shrimp for 1 minute, stirring. Add the garlic powder and butter, and continue cooking for 2 minutes. Add the wine and the lemon juice, then the milk to thicken (you can forego the milk if you don't want to thicken the sauce). Cook for 4 more minutes, then serve hot. Serves 6.

SCALLOPS, OYSTERS, AND CLAMS

Scallops and Mushrooms Gorgonzola

Jess's Market, Rockland, Maine

ALFREDO SAUCE

2 tablespoons (¼ stick) butter

2 tablespoons flour

1 cup milk (whole or low fat)

1 garlic cloves, finely chopped

Salt and pepper to taste

¼ cup Parmesan cheese, grated

2 tablespoons olive oil

½ package (4 ounces) fresh
    mushrooms (halved if large)

½ onion, finely chopped

1 pound scallops

¼ cup dry white wine

Fresh or dried parsley leaves/flakes

Juice of ½ lemon

2 ounces Gorgonzola cheese,
    crumbled

1 package Pepperidge Farm
    stuffing mix

1 pound cooked pasta (optional)

This recipe from Jess's Market calls for just a small amount of Gorgonzola, which adds a very nice, subtle flavor to this baked scallop dish.

Preheat the oven to 375 degrees.

To make the Alfredo sauce, melt the butter in a pot. Mix in the flour and stir until well blended, then add the milk and stir until thickened. Add the garlic, salt, and pepper, and continue to stir. Melt the Parmesan cheese by adding slowly to the sauce. Stir well until thoroughly blended.

In a nonstick frying pan, brown the mushrooms well in the olive oil. Add the onion and scallops and cook just until the onions are translucent and the scallops are slightly browned. Add the wine, parsley, lemon juice, and more salt and pepper to taste. Heat through.

Pour the scallop mixture into a shallow casserole dish, and cover with the Alfredo sauce. Sprinkle on the Gorgonzola cheese, then top with a light coating of stuffing mix. Bake in the preheated oven for 15 minutes or until the top is golden brown. Serve over cooked pasta, if desired. Makes 4 to 6 servings.

Scalloped Oysters

R&D Seafood, Woonsocket, Rhode Island

1 pint shucked oysters

2 cups Ritz or Townhouse crackers, crushed to a medium or coarse consistency

½ cup (1 stick) butter, melted

Pepper to taste

¾ cup light cream

¼ cup oyster liquor, from the shucked oysters

¼ teaspoon Worcestershire sauce

½ teaspoon salt

This recipe from R&D Seafood is very much like an oyster casserole, rich with butter, cream, and fresh-shucked oyster goodness.

Preheat the oven to 350 degrees. Drain the oysters, reserving ¼ cup of the liquor. Combine the crumbs and the butter.

Spread ⅓ of the butter and crumbs mixture in a shallow casserole dish. Cover with half of the oysters and season with pepper to taste. Use another ⅓ of the butter and crumbs mixture and spread a second layer, then cover with the remaining oysters.

In a small bowl, combine the cream, oyster liquor, Worcestershire sauce, and salt. Pour the mixture over the top layer of oysters, then top with the remaining butter and crumbs. Bake for about 40 minutes or until the top is golden brown. Serves 2 to 3.

Bud's Fish Market

Branford, Connecticut

Bud's is one of the biggest and best-known seafood markets east of New Haven on the Connecticut shoreline. In the Indian Neck section of Branford, Bud's serves the locals and cottage renters of this elegantly scruffy shoreline enclave, as well as customers well beyond the boundaries of the neighborhood and even the town. There are a couple of reasons for this: first, it's a top-flight retail market with a 30-foot display case of fresh seafood and other delights; second, it's been owned by the same family since 1948, with second-generation owner Hal Beckley (pictured on the next page) behind the market counter nearly every day.

Bud's is housed in a long, narrow building that appears outsized for the smallish, quaint neighborhood setting. Inside is a long, seafood-stuffed stainless steel and glass counter with green-shaded conical lamps shedding warm light over the offerings. Denizens of Indian Neck are fortunate indeed to have such a first-class seafood emporium close by, and

energetic owner Beckley is more often than not found right at the counter with two or three helpers, ready to answer your seafood questions and wrap up any fish or shellfish that strike your fancy.

Bud's is one of those quality markets that cuts its fish fresh every day. Whole fish are delivered regularly, and Hal and his crew hand-cut fillets in the back room as they're needed in the display case or for special order. This is one of the signs of a quality shop. Not every fish market can do this, but the quantity of business at Bud's is such that they can offer this important service to their customers.

The display case is divided into two units, with most of the fresh fish fillets on the right-hand side, and much of the shellfish and prepared foods on the left. It's easy to come in with the intention of buying a pound of haddock or cod and walking out with a couple bags full of fresh and prepared seafood delights.

Lining the walls next to and opposite the display cases are an array of seasonings, pastas, grains, cooking utensils, and other enticing and useful items for any seafood feast. On the right side of the retail room are a few large, bubbling aquamarine tanks holding Bud's inventory of lobsters. Taking a page from the numerous lobster pounds in Maine, Bud's will ship live lobsters overnight anywhere in the country, keeping the lobsters (or other fresh seafood) cool and alive with special stay-cool packs in each container.

Hal is a hard-working owner who's on top of his business at all times, and that's the key to success in running a seafood market. Those who put in the time and the effort reap the rewards of loyal customers, who keep coming back again and again. It helps explain how such an outsized seafood market can thrive and prosper in a relatively small community, well off the beaten path.

Hal Beckley

Sea Scallops a la Bud's

Bud's Fish Market, Branford, Connecticut

18 large (or diver-caught) sea scallops, cut in half

1½ cups breadcrumbs

1 garlic clove, minced

2 tablespoons fresh parsley, chopped

2 tablespoons olive oil

3 tablespoons (⅜ stick) butter

¼ cup white wine

¼ cup lemon juice

6 scallop shells, warmed in the oven (for serving)

Coat the scallops with the breadcrumbs, and set aside.

In a large pan or skillet, sauté the garlic and parsley in the olive oil and butter over medium-high heat. Add the breaded scallops and gently fry until browned (just a few minutes—don't overcook).

Add the white wine and lemon juice. Continue cooking gently for a few minutes until most of the wine evaporates. Place the scallops in the heated shells (or other small containers), and serve hot. Serves 4.

Bud's Deviled Stuffed Clams

Bud's Fish Market, Branford, Connecticut

14 large quahog clams

1 onion, chopped

10 saltine crackers, crushed

Salt and pepper to taste

Pinch of dry mustard

1 egg, beaten

Clam broth (reserved from steaming clams)

Butter or salt pork

Using a covered pot, steam the clams in 2 inches of water until the shells open. Carefully remove the clams from the pot using tongs, and reserve the broth. Allow the clams to sit until they are cool to the touch.

Remove the clam meat from the shells and mince. Set the shells aside for serving.

Preheat the oven to 375 degrees. In a mixing bowl, combine the chopped clams, the chopped onion, crackers, salt, pepper, mustard, and beaten egg, and then drizzle in some of the clam broth to create a sticky consistency. Place a rounded lump of the sticky clam mixture in the middle of each clam shell. Put a small pat of butter (or small piece of salt pork) on each clam, and place the stuffed clams on a cookie sheet. Bake in the oven until nicely browned, about 18 to 22 minutes. Serves 4.

Oysters Flanders

Flanders Fish Market, East Lyme, Connecticut

16 oysters, in their shells

1 cup (2 sticks) butter, melted

2 cups spicy Italian sausage, cooked and minced

2 cups shredded pepper jack cheese

2 lemons, cut into wedges

Flanders founder and owner Paul Formica believes that seafood and spicy "go together." He came up with this unusual combination of briny oysters, creamy cheese, and spicy sausage—his own variation on Oysters Rockefeller, with a kick to it!

Preheat the oven to 400 degrees. Rinse the oysters in cold water to remove any sand or other debris on the shells. Shuck the oysters with an oyster-shucking knife, being careful to keep them cup-side up, to retain as much of the oyster liquid as possible.

Place the opened oysters in a single layer on a large baking sheet. Drizzle each oyster with 1 tablespoon of melted butter. Top each oyster with 2 tablespoons of minced sausage, then 2 tablespoons of cheese.

Place the baking sheet in the oven, and bake for 10 to 12 minutes, until the oysters and toppings are bubbling. Serve immediately with lemon wedges. Serves 8 for appetizers or 4 for dinner.

Bay Scallops Provençal

Nauset Fish and Lobster Pool, Orleans, Massachusetts

1 pound bay scallops

Salt and pepper

¼ cup all-purpose flour

¼ cup (½ stick) unsalted butter, divided

½ cup chopped shallots

1 clove garlic, minced

¼ cup fresh parsley, chopped

⅓ cup white wine

1 lemon

Bay scallops are a seasonal specialty on Cape Cod and the islands, and are only available fresh from late fall through winter. This simple recipe brings out the essence of these delicacies, and their mild flavor pairs well with simple vegetable, potato, or rice sides, or with a salad with vinaigrette dressing.

Sprinkle the scallops lightly with salt and pepper. Toss them in the flour, and shake off the excess.

In a large sauté pan, melt 2 tablespoons of butter until sizzling. Add the scallops in one layer, until each browns lightly on one side. Turn the scallops and brown on the other side.

Add the shallots, garlic, and parsley, and melt in the remaining butter. Sauté for 2 minutes, then add the wine. Serve hot with lemon slices. Serves 2 to 3.

Scalloped Scallops

Port Lobster Company, Kennebunkport, Maine

1 pint sea scallops

1 cup cracker crumbs

½ cup breadcrumbs

½ cup (1 stick) butter, melted

⅔ cup cream

1½ cups grated cheddar cheese

Ever hear of scalloped potatoes? Here's a recipe for scalloped scallops, a redundancy that you'll find will be most welcome at your dinner table.

Wash and pick over the scallops, then cut them into small pieces. Mix the cracker crumbs and breadcrumbs together. Add the melted butter to the crumb mixture and combine thoroughly.

Preheat the oven to 350 degrees. Put a layer of buttered crumbs in a lightly greased baking dish. Cover with half the chopped scallops. Add half the cream, and top with half the cheese. Repeat the layering of buttered crumbs, scallops, cream, and cheese, topping off with any remaining buttered crumbs. Bake for about 60 minutes, or until golden brown and firm on top. Serves 4.

Turner's Seafood

Gloucester, Massachusetts

Jim Turner

"Anything fresher still swims" is the catch-phrase at Turner's Seafood Market in the historic fishing town of Gloucester, Massachusetts. If you're going to be in the seafood game in this town, your fish had better be fresh, and Turner's—with its seafood market, its wholesale fish business, and its restaurants in nearby Salem and Melrose—more than lives up to expectations.

Turner's roots lie deep in the Boston-area wholesale seafood trade, and their retail market came to be as a sort of wonderful afterthought. Founder James "Jim" Turner arrived in Boston in 1920 from Canada and began working on the Boston Fish Pier. Learning the business inside and out over the next few decades, he eventually opened Turner Fisheries, a wholesale fish business, in 1954. Turner's got in early on the advancements in food transport in the mid-1900s, and they capitalized on air shipments of their fresh seafood to points west and south all over the United States. Soon, Turner's had an enviable yet well-earned national reputation for offering the highest quality New England seafood.

In 1989, Jim's son, John, created a new wholesale operation in Gloucester and named it J. Turner Seafoods, Inc. The new business was created in response to the changing seafood market and reduced fish stocks. Located only several blocks from Gloucester's commercial fishing docks, the Turners continued to focus on their wholesale business. But their operation caught the attention of locals, who kept stopping in and asking if they could buy some fresh fish direct from the plant. Enough such requests eventually prompted the Turners to open a retail market in the 1990s, as an offshoot of the wholesale processing plant. James's grandson Jim was put in charge of the market, which he still runs to this day, along with his other management duties within the Turner empire.

Housed in a 1½-story, shingled, shack-like building, Turner's Seafood Market has all the charm of an old-fashioned New England fish operation. There's a chalkboard affixed to the wall next to the front door, announcing what's in the seafood cases that day. All the fish comes directly from the adjacent processing plant, meaning it's fresh off the boat that morning. Standard offerings in the fish and shellfish cases include tuna, swordfish, cod, haddock, halibut, jumbo shrimp, and fresh-picked Jonah crabmeat. Live lobsters are kept in a tank in full sight just inside the front door, and Turner's will be happy to cook them up for you.

Turner's restaurants in Salem and Melrose also have their own small fresh-fish markets. In addition, they keep the Gloucester retail market stocked with lots of prepared foods from their kitchens, including shrimp cocktails, crab cakes, chowders, bisques, and prepared lunches and dinners from the restaurants' menus. It's a nice, symbiotic relationship, with delivery trucks going between the outlets throughout the day.

Turner's is one of the biggest names in the Boston-area seafood market, doing business with many of the best-known restaurants and retailers in the region. You'll be doing yourself a favor by availing yourself of the goodies in their markets and at their restaurants.

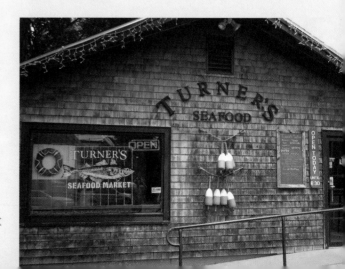

Turner's Stuffed Clams

Turner's Seafood, Gloucester, Massachusetts

6 large cherrystone clams

3 strips bacon, cooked and crumbled

¼ cup onion, minced

¼ cup celery, minced

1 clove garlic, diced

2 tablespoons (¼ stick) butter

1 can (or 8 ounces fresh) chopped clams

2 sleeves Ritz crackers, crushed

¼ cup grated Parmesan cheese

¼ cup parsley, chopped rough

Juice of 1 lemon, plus lemon slices for garnish

Hot sauce

Shuck the cherrystone clams carefully, removing the clams from their shells and reserving the liquid. Chop the clams up and set the chopped cherrystones and liquid aside. Clean the 12 shell halves thoroughly.

Cook the bacon in a skillet and then and drain on paper towels, reserving the bacon grease in the pan. Crumble the bacon and set it aside.

Over medium heat, sauté the onion, celery, and garlic in the skillet with some of the bacon grease. Once the onion and celery soften (about 2 minutes), add the butter and crumbled bacon. Allow the butter to melt, then add the chopped cherrystone clams and juice and the rest of the clams, and simmer for three minutes.

Transfer the contents of the pan to a large mixing bowl. Add the crushed Ritz crackers, the Parmesan cheese, the parsley, and the lemon juice. Mix thoroughly and allow the mixture to cool.

Preheat the oven to 450 degrees. Fill the cleaned shells with the stuffing, being careful not to pack the stuffing in too tightly. Put the shells on cookie sheets, and bake in the oven until golden on top. Serve with lemon and hot sauce. Serves 3 to 4.

Bud's Scalloped Oysters

Bud's Fish Market, Branford, Connecticut

½ cup (1 stick) butter

3 cups cracker crumbs

Salt and pepper to taste

1 pint shucked oysters, drained

1½ cups milk

This makes a great side dish at Thanksgiving dinner. It's like having an extra version of turkey stuffing on the table.

Preheat the oven to 350 degrees.

Melt the butter in a medium-size pot, using medium heat. Stir in the cracker crumbs, then add the salt and pepper to taste (salt lightly, as oysters are naturally salty).

Add the oysters and milk to the pot, stirring to combine with the butter and cracker crumbs. Pour the mixture into a baking dish and bake for about 1 hour, until golden brown on top. Serves 4 as a side dish.

NEW ENGLAND EXOTICA

Atlantic Seafood

Old Saybrook, Connecticut

Sometimes an abiding passion for the sea (and seafood) inspires someone to get into the seafood business. Such is not the case with Lisa Friedman, owner of Atlantic Seafood, in Old Saybrook, Connecticut. For purely pragmatic reasons, Lisa was shopping around for a business that would keep her closer to home and get her out of the furniture and real estate businesses that no longer held her interest. Prior to purchasing the shop, the closest Lisa and her husband had come to selling seafood was catching mako sharks in Long Island Sound for sport, and selling them to fishermen in Montauk to help defray their boat fuel costs.

Ten years after taking over Atlantic Seafood Market, Friedman has fallen in love with the business and built an excellent store that consistently wins awards as the best place to get fresh seafood in the lower Connecticut River valley. This whitewashed roadside stand with its bright red awning is chock-full of excellent seafood surprises—from its award-winning cold lobster roll to its in-house, freshly cut fish fillets, to wonderful seasonal specials on such local favorites as shad, blackfish, smelts, and scungilli.

In addition to Friedman's tireless efforts to make Atlantic Seafood as good as it can be, much of the credit also goes to resident chef Jerry Doran, a Culinary Institute of America–trained seafood specialist who has worked in a number of four- and five-star restaurants in the New York area. Guided by the philosophy that "less is more," Doran finds joy in creating simple dishes and prepared foods, which occupy fully half of Atlantic Seafood's display cases and much of their freezer space. Here you'll find such seafood (and non-seafood) treats as cod cakes, crab or lobster ravioli, swordfish cakes, tuna cakes, Carolina coleslaw, and seaweed salad.

Atlantic Seafood was one of the early adopters of the wood-plank method of grilling of fish. There are always several varieties of wood planks to choose from in the store—everything from hickory to alder to olive to cherry, as well as the ever-popular cedar and mesquite. Purchase a plank, soak it for several hours in water, daub it with olive oil, and it's all set to go over medium heat on a charcoal or propane outdoor grill. A particularly nice dish for this method of cooking is fresh ahi tuna covered with Char-Crust ginger teriyaki rub.

There are all sorts of other fun things happening at Atlantic Seafood throughout the year. During Lent, Lisa will hold seafood-cooking demonstrations in the market. Jerry and a couple of the other fine cooks at Atlantic prepare and explain simple and innovative dishes to serve to family and friends during the pre-Easter season. Come spring, Atlantic goes crazy for shad. Local shad fishermen on the Connecticut River bring in their daily catch of fillets and roe for as long as the shad are running up the river.

Come summer, it's lobster time, and Atlantic Seafood rolls out its Lobster Bake in a Can. For a set price, you may pick up a big can that contains a hard-shelled lobster, corn on the cob, fingerling potatoes, and a choice of clams or mussels. Take the can home, add a few cups of water, and heat on the stove or grill for half an hour or so for your own summertime lobster feast. (All Atlantic Seafood asks is that you return the can!)

Atlantic Seafood has really lit up the seafood scene in Old Saybrook and surrounding communities over the past decade. It serves as a model for how to make seafood the fun and healthy cuisine it is.

Baked Shad

Atlantic Seafood, Old Saybrook, Connecticut

1½ pounds shad fillets

Salt

Black pepper

Juice of 1 lemon

¼ cup white wine

3 to 4 butter pats

Hot sauce (optional—a small amount will increase the flavor without adding heat)

In late spring and early summer, when the shad are running on the nearby Connecticut River, Atlantic Seafood is a beehive of activity, selling and preparing fresh shad fillets and shad roe, procured daily from local fishermen. Locals love this seasonal treat, and it's gaining in popularity throughout New England. This basic baking recipe is a great entrée to the world of shad.

Preheat the oven to 375 degrees. Place the shad fillets, skin side down, in a shallow baking dish. Lightly salt and pepper the fillets, and pour the lemon juice on top. Add a splash of white wine, then put the pats of butter on top of the fillets.

Bake for 15 to 20 minutes, until the shad is just done, flaking easily with the touch of a fork. Use the liquid in the baking dish as a sauce. Remove the fillets and spoon the sauce over the fish. Add a few dashes of hot sauce to the fish sauce before spooning, if desired. Serves 3 to 4.

(Shad roe is also very tasty when prepared like this. Just substitute the shad fillets with shad roe, and adjust all the ingredients according to the weight of the roe. Serve with a crispy, crumbled bacon topping.)

Shad Roe

Atlantic Seafood, Old Saybrook, Connecticut

1 pair shad roe

½ cup heavy cream

Salt and pepper to taste

Juice of 1 lemon

Hot sauce to taste

½ cup flour

1 tablespoon olive oil

Once you've acquired a taste for baked shad, it's time to move up to the more complicated flavor of shad roe. The roe of a female shad is rather immense, resembling a pair of elongated livers. The preferred cooking method involves searing the roe on the stovetop, initially, then carefully transferring and baking the roe in the oven.

Preheat the oven to 375 degrees. Marinate the roe in the heavy cream, salt, pepper, lemon juice, and hot sauce for 20 minutes. Lightly dredge the roe in the flour.

Heat the olive oil in a pan over medium heat. Brown the roe in the pan, 1 to 2 minutes per side, being careful not to break the membrane. Carefully remove the roe from the pan, transfer to a baking dish, and bake in the preheated oven for 6 to 8 minutes, until firm and just cooked through. Serves 3 to 4.

Essex Shad Bake

For more than fifty years, the Rotary Club of Essex, Connecticut—a lovely town on the banks of the Connecticut River—has been holding a very unusual and highly entertaining shad bake.

What is a shad bake? Let's begin with the shad. American shad is a fish species that spends most of its adult life in and around the waters of the north Atlantic. Shad are anadromous, which means that, in the spring, they swim upriver in order to spawn, then return to the ocean for another year. Adult shad typically weigh between three and eight pounds and are usually more than a foot long.

Shad has been described as the "fish that fed the nation's founders," as it was a highly popular dish in colonial times. An entire fishing culture and industry sprang up each spring, with fishermen dragging their nets upriver after dark to ensnare spawning shad by the thousands.

The shad stock has dwindled dramatically in recent years, but many native New Englanders still enjoy the several weeks, from early May to mid-June, that shad are available in local seafood markets. In addition to the shad fillets, the roe from female shad—a large, liver-like mass—is considered a delicacy among shad aficionados.

Back to the shad bake. Each year in early June, the Rotarians in Essex sponsor a shad festival of sorts. The one-day event recently moved to the grounds of the Connecticut River Museum, right where the foot of Main Street meets the banks of the namesake river.

A large wood-fed fire pit is built in an open field next to the museum, and is kept blazing for several hours while a small army of volunteers prepares the shad for baking. Preparations include nailing the shad fillets to wooden planks and seasoning the fillets with olive oil and paprika. The planks are then positioned in circular fashion around the scorching fire, where they slowly bake for fifteen to twenty minutes in the searing heat. When a

batch of fillets are ready, a call goes up from one of the Rotarians, the planks are pulled away from the fire, and the nails are removed from the planks, freeing up the fillets for hungry customers under a nearby open-air tent.

There are lots of fun things to take in while waiting for the fillets to bake, such as a fascinating demonstration on how to fillet a shad. The fish has hundreds of small bones, and it's an increasingly rare skill to be able to fillet shad quickly and efficiently. It's also fun to watch the fillets being nailed to and removed from the planks using a pneumatic carpenter's tool designed to remove nails from roofs and other construction projects.

The best part, of course, is sitting down to a plate of shad, a simple tossed salad, and a slice of locally baked pie, accompanied by a glass of beer or wine. There's nothing quite like the Essex Shad Bake, and it's well worth the trip to this charming Connecticut River town to take it all in.

Baked Bluefish with Dijon Mustard Sauce

Turner's Seafood, Gloucester, Massachusetts

2 7-ounce bluefish fillets

½ cup mayonnaise

¼ cup Dijon mustard

1 tablespoon horseradish

1 teaspoon Worcestershire sauce

1 tablespoon lemon juice

1 tablespoon shallots, minced

This is a classic New England preparation. The tangy sauce complements and tempers the natural oiliness of bluefish.

Preheat the oven to 375 degrees. Place the bluefish fillets in a baking dish and roast them in the oven for 6 minutes, until they're a little more than halfway cooked.

Whisk together all the remaining ingredients to make the mustard sauce. Generously coat the par-cooked bluefish with the sauce, and return the fish to the oven to finish cooking. The mustard sauce should caramelize slightly on top, and the fish fillet should flake at the touch of a fork. Remove from the oven, and serve with a side such as a salad, vegetable, or rice. Serves 2.

Sanders Fish Market

Portsmouth, New Hampshire

This may be one of the prettiest fish markets in all of New England. Housed in a lavender-colored, two-story colonial frame building on a back channel of the Piscataqua River, Sanders Fish Market could fit very easily into the middle of Portsmouth's historic Strawbery Banke neighborhood. It's warm and inviting from the street, and even more so once you pass through its front door into the sun-splashed seafood market and cafe.

Behold the fresh seafood cases before you, about twenty feet away, across a polished wooden floor adorned with a

SANDERS FISH MARKET area rug. In those cases you'll find such staples as tuna and swordfish steaks, locally caught haddock, halibut, and flounder, and hake and pollock from the Gulf of Maine. Hook-and-line-caught cod from Iceland is regularly featured, as are such tropical favorites as snapper and grouper, each flown in fresh from South American waters.

On the shellfish front, day-boat sea scallops are popular with the locals, as are all the fresh clam varieties, including steamers, littlenecks, and razor necks, and a constantly changing variety of fresh, live oysters. Softshell crabs from the Chesapeake Bay are available during the warmer months, and fresh-picked Jonah crabmeat is stocked regularly.

In addition to all the fresh seafood, Sanders cooks up fresh batches of chowder and seafood stews every day, which you can take with you or enjoy at one of the café tables in the spacious store. Sandwiches, including Sanders's famous lobster roll, are also for sale. There's fresh-brewed coffee, home-baked pies, and other desserts available throughout the day.

Sander Fish Market is the offspring of the Sanders Lobster Company, which was founded in 1954 by Earle Sanders, the patriarch of the Sanders seafood clan. The Sanders family's main business is still lobster wholesaling, which they do primarily from a dock on Pray Street, not far from the fish market.

Earle's son Jim bought the fish market from another local seafood family in 1987 and passed it along to his son Michael in 2008, the same year that Earle passed away. Since that time, Sanders Fish Market has flourished as one of the brightest retail stars in Portsmouth.

Needless to say, the fish market is well stocked at all times with lobsters. You may buy them in any of a variety of sizes, and Sanders will cook or par-cook (half-cook) them for you for a small charge. If you just want the good stuff and to avoid all the cracking and picking, there's always plenty of fresh-picked lobster meat available in the seafood case.

As if all this weren't enough, each Friday Jim's sister (Michael's aunt) Kristin—who has been in the business for decades—drives the company truck up to Concord, New Hampshire, and sells fresh seafood out of the back to the appreciative inland crowd. She claims to have over a hundred regular customers who eagerly await her arrival at the Concord Arena.

The Sanders family truly has a seafood dynasty in the best sense of the term, and the people in Portsmouth (and Concord) are very fortunate to have such a longstanding purveyor and steward of the community in their midst. Help reward them by paying Sanders Fish Market a visit the next time you're in town.

Halibut Puttanesca

Sanders Fish Market, Portsmouth, New Hampshire

1½ cups marinara or tomato sauce

4 garlic cloves, minced

½ cup green olives, chopped

3 tablespoons capers, drained

½ cup red wine

2 teaspoons anchovy paste

4 5-ounce halibut fillets

Kosher salt and freshly ground
    black pepper, to taste

¼ cup fresh basil leaves, chopped

Puttanesca is a Neapolitan tomato sauce most frequently associated with spaghetti and other pasta dishes, but it works perfectly well in this stovetop recipe for halibut.

Pour the tomato sauce into a large saucepan and begin warming over medium heat. Add the garlic, olives, capers, wine, and anchovy paste. Bring the mixture to a steaming simmer for 5 minutes, still over medium heat, stirring occasionally.

Season the halibut on both sides with salt and pepper. Add the halibut fillets to the sauce. Cover and simmer for 3 to 5 minutes, until the fish is fork tender. Sprinkle with fresh basil. Serves 4.

Baked Breaded Tilapia

City Fish Market, Wethersfield, Connecticut

1 cup breadcrumbs

1 tablespoon grated Parmesan cheese

1 teaspoon oregano or Italian seasoning

½ teaspoon salt

¼ teaspoon black pepper

2–3 tablespoons vegetable oil

1½ pounds tilapia fillets

Tilapia is a farmed freshwater fish that's low in fat and mild in flavor. It's suited to many different cooking methods, but this recipe for breaded fillets—baked up crisp and tender in the oven—is one of the favorites at City Fish Market, in Wethersfield, Connecticut.

Preheat the oven to 375 degrees and lightly oil a baking sheet. In a plastic or paper bag, combine the breadcrumbs, Parmesan cheese, oregano (or Italian seasoning), salt, and pepper. Hold the top of the bag shut and shake to mix everything together.

Pour the vegetable oil into a small bowl. Working with one fillet at a time, brush both sides with a little of the oil, then drop the fillet into the bag with the breadcrumb mixture and shake to coat well. Remove the fillet from the bag and place on the prepared baking sheet. Repeat with the remaining fillets.

Bake for 10 minutes, turn the fillets over, and continue to bake for another 5 to 10 minutes, or until the fish flakes with a fork. Serves 4.

Easy Baked Maple-Glazed Arctic Char

City Fish Market, Wethersfield, Connecticut

3 tablespoons maple syrup

1½ teaspoons cornstarch, dissolved in 1 tablespoon water

2 tablespoons soy sauce

1 tablespoon ginger, fresh grated

4 fresh Arctic char fillets (about 6 ounces each)

1 scallion, sliced thin (white part plus about 2–3 inches of the green)

1 tablespoon toasted sliced almonds (optional)

This Arctic char recipe is a delicious, simple, and afford-able dish to make.

Preheat the oven to 450 degrees. In a small bowl, whisk together the maple syrup, cornstarch solution, soy sauce, and ginger until smooth and blended. Place the Arctic char fillets skin-side down in a shallow baking pan, and pour the syrup mixture over the Arctic char.

Bake for about 15 to 18 minutes, basting with the syrup mixture in the pan halfway through the cooking process. Make sure the fish flakes easily with a fork. Sprinkle the cooked fillets with scallions and almonds before serving. Serves 4.

Friendly Fisherman

North Eastham, Massachusetts

"Friendly" is the perfect word to describe this charming North Eastham seafood market, just 20 miles south of Provincetown on the outer reaches of Cape Cod. Not far from the Cape Cod National Seashore Visitors' Center, the Friendly Fisherman holds an enviable spot both geographically and in the hearts and minds of Cape Cod locals and frequent visitors. It's one of those places that are easy to reach and—once you're there—hard to leave.

Janet Demetri and her husband, Michael, bought the market back in 1989 and quickly became known for their consistently fresh fish. They established good connections with many of the local fishermen, which helped them gain credibility and build a solid, loyal customer base from the beginning. The Demetris' daughter, Alana, was born that inaugural year.

A few years later, a small dine-in-the-rough seafood operation was built on the side of the cottage-size market, and Michael began living his dream of putting his culinary education to good use in a quality eatery. In 2006, Michael succumbed to cancer, and Alana, then a teenager, stepped in to give her mom a hand with the business. The two of them continue to run the Friendly Fisherman to this day.

The first thing that strikes you upon entering the market is how homey and cozy it is. The wood-framed seafood cases with hinged glass doors were custom-built by Michael in the 1990s, as were the wooden side tables and bins filled with fresh produce, much of it locally grown. Fresh-baked pies and breads line another table.

On to the seafood. The Friendly Fisherman's relations with the local fishermen remain very good, and the fishermen often save the best of their catch for the market's cases. Janet, Alana, and their crew hand-cut the fillets from all the fish they purchase, and because they are only in the retail business (no wholesaling to other retail customers), they have a very tight control over their inventory, and are able to keep their offerings extremely fresh.

Among the locally harvested goodies to be found regularly at Friendly Fisherman are native harpooned swordfish cut into thick steaks for the grill, sushi-grade tuna, and fresh cod and scrod from down the road in Chatham. Bluefish and striped bass (whole or filleted) are to be found in season, as well. Local flounder and native scallops are other favorites and available throughout most of the season.

Lobster is a big seller here, also. The Fisherman's large tanks can hold up to 2,000 pounds of lobsters of every conceivable size, from 1-pound "chickens" to behemoth 8- to 10-pounders. Two lobster boats service the fish market almost exclusively, and they fish the "back side" (ocean side) of the Cape by Provincetown, where the biggest and best lobsters are to be found. If you wish, the market will cook, crack, and split your lobsters for take-out and enjoyment at home.

If you get a chance, grab some lunch or dinner at the adjoining shack, where all sorts of deep-fried fare is available, along with whole, cooked lobsters and an amazing lobster roll that always has a piece or two of claw meat on the top. The open-air shack is a BYOB operation, and it even has a small play area for kids.

While nearby operations may be larger and sometimes busier in the summer months, the Friendly Fisherman lends a bit of that old-time, small-town Cape Cod look and feel from days gone by. It's well worth a visit and worthy of your patronage.

Baked Bluefish for the Grill or Oven

The Friendly Fisherman, North Eastham, Massachusetts

1 skinned bluefish fillet,
approximately 6–8 ounces

Mayonnaise

½ onion, diced

½ green pepper, diced

½ red pepper, diced

Salt, pepper, and lemon juice to
taste

One of the keys to cooking up really good bluefish is to get it as fresh as possible. Short of catching the bluefish yourself, your local seafood market is the best bet for getting the freshest possible fillets. This recipe, from the Friendly Fisherman on the outer reaches of Cape Cod, calls for wrapping the bluefish in aluminum foil with a bunch of fresh, chopped vegetables for a meal in a packet.

Place the bluefish fillet in foil large enough to seal it up completely. Spread the mayonnaise over the entire fillet. Add the onion and pepper. Sprinkle the salt, pepper, and lemon juice over the top. Seal the foil loosely, creating a packet. Place the packet on a medium-high grill for 25 minutes, or bake in a preheated oven at 350 degrees for 25 minutes. The fish will be light in color, flaky, and fork-tender when done. Serves 1 (create more individual packets for additional servings).

Fisherman's Catch

Damariscotta, Maine

Smack dab in the middle of Damariscotta, Maine's charming Main Street is the equally charming storefront fish market named Fisherman's Catch. It sits close to the bridge spanning the Damariscotta River, and is surrounded by eateries, taverns, coffee shops, municipal buildings, and churches, all lined up along the old Route 1.

Though there has been a seafood market in this location for close to fifty years, Fisherman's Catch didn't come into being until 2013, when Heath Reed became the new owner. Fisherman's Catch prides itself on being a small, hands-on market that has a great reputation with the locals. Lots of people in Damariscotta won't shop anywhere else for their fish.

Why not? First and perhaps foremost, most of the fish is locally caught and hand-filleted on the cutting table just behind the seafood case. Second, the staff consists mainly of seasoned fishermen and others with lots of experience catching and handling fish and shellfish. Of particular note here are the oysters harvested from the Damariscotta River and the clams that are harvested from the river flats at low tide. There's also lots of frozen seafood and plenty of live lobsters in their tank at all times. The staff will cook your lobsters for you, if you wish, and it'll set you back the princely sum of 75 cents per lobster.

Check this place out to see what fish markets were like in their prime, when there were at least two or three in every city and town along the New England seaboard. It's a blessed throwback to an earlier time, when small-scale retailing and friendly, personalized service were the rule of the day.

Corned Hake and Potatoes

Fisherman's Catch Seafood Market, Damariscotta, Maine

1½ pounds hake

Salt pork

1 small onion, diced

4 medium potatoes

1 tablespoon vinegar

This storefront fish market on Main Street in downtown Damariscotta, Maine, cuts its fillets right behind the counter for the freshest fish you can get. This hearty dish is particularly good in the colder months, when protein and carbohydrates are needed to help battle the elements.

Salt the hake fillets and set them aside for 1 hour. Dice the salt pork and onion, and fry over medium heat in a skillet. Then set them aside.

In one pot of boiling water, cook the potatoes until they can be mashed, approximately 15 minutes. In another pot of boiling water, cook the hake for 15 minutes, and remove carefully.

Mash the potatoes in a large bowl. Add the hake, salt pork scraps, onion, and vinegar, and mix together, using a large spoon. Serve with steamed vegetables. Serves 4.

Easy Snapper Parmesan

R&D Seafood, Woonsocket, Rhode Island

3 red snapper fillets, 6 to 8 ounces each

⅓ cup mayonnaise

¼ cup plus 2 tablespoons grated Parmesan cheese

1 small onion, finely chopped

1 garlic clove, minced

2 tablespoons parsley, chopped

½ teaspoon salt

¼ teaspoon pepper

Lemon wedges, for garnish

Preheat the oven to 425 degrees. Arrange snapper fillets in a single layer on a lightly oiled baking dish or cookie sheet.

In a small bowl, combine the mayonnaise, ¼ cup Parmesan cheese, onion, garlic, parsley, salt, and pepper. Spread the mixture evenly over the snapper fillets. Sprinkle the remaining 2 tablespoons of Parmesan cheese over the top.

Bake 10 minutes, or until the fish begins to flake when tested with a fork and the Parmesan cheese is slightly browned. Serve immediately, and garnish with lemon wedges. Serves 3.

Simple, Easy Striped Bass

The Friendly Fisherman, North Eastham, Massachusetts

1 skinned striped bass fillet
(¾ pound to 1½ pounds works
best)

1 bottle Thousand Island salad
dressing (any bottled version
is fine)

When it comes to cooking, simple methods are often the best, and such is the case with this easy way to prepare tender, succulent striped bass, using a foil packet on the grill.

Place the bass fillet on a piece of aluminum foil large enough to seal it up completely. Cover the fillet liberally with the salad dressing. Seal the foil loosely over the fillet and dressing, creating a packet. Place on the grill over medium high heat for 25 minutes or until the fish flakes easily with a fork.
Serves 2 to 4.

Branzino in Parchment

New Deal Fish Market, Cambridge, Massachusetts

1 whole branzino (approximately 1 pound), scaled and insides removed (You may wish to have this done at the fish market.)

Pinch of salt

Pinch of crushed black pepper

2 tablespoons extra-virgin olive oil

¼ cup dry white wine

1 teaspoon fennel seeds

Also known as European seabass, branzino (its Italian name) is a popular fish in Mediterranean countries. It has firm, white flesh and few bones, making it ideal for cooking whole.

Preheat the oven to 450 degrees. Rub the scaled, gutted fish with salt, black pepper, and olive oil. Make sure to also rub the salt, black pepper, and olive oil on the inner cavity of the fish. Place the fish on a large sheet of parchment paper, and add the white wine and fennel seeds. Drizzle a small amount of olive oil on the fish, if desired.

Place the branzino in sealed parchment paper (see tip below), then place in a baking pan or dish and bake for approximately 15 minutes. Remove the fish from the parchment paper by cutting the paper with scissors (being careful not to be burned by the hot steam that may escape). Serve with any green vegetable and your choice of rice or potatoes. Serves 2.

Tip: The parchment paper must be large enough to envelop and seal in the entire fish. The branzino will cook in the parchment paper, which must be sealed to prevent the ingredients from leaking out. Think of the parchment paper as a bag that you will place the fish in and that you will seal around the edges before cooking.

Harbor Fish Market

Portland, Maine

This is the fish market by which all other New England seafood markets should be measured. Harbor Fish is a venerable, old school fish emporium, complete with wood clapboard exterior, concrete floors, tables of fish and shellfish on ice, and a real open-market look and feel throughout. Its 50-plus linear feet of display cases of fresh fish and shellfish lend credence to the assertion that this is the best seafood market in New England.

Harbor Fish began its life in 1969, when Ben Alfiero Sr. and his brother John took over the seafood market at historic 9 Custom House Wharf, in Portland, and renamed it Harbor Fish

Market. John passed his share of the business to Ben in 1975, and over the next few years Ben's sons Nick, Ben Jr., and Mike joined their father in the family business.

The four Alfieros began expanding the business in a number of directions, supplying restaurants, processing seafood for national food chains, and wholesaling to a variety of retail customers. Today, Nick is president of Harbor Fish, presiding over a broad array of activities, including Harbor Fish's award-winning seafood market.

Custom House Wharf is a part of the Portland waterfront that time has forgotten—and that's a good thing. Unlike other

nearby wharfs, which have been spiffed up for the tourist trade, Custom House Wharf is a walk back through time, offering a glimpse of what a real working wharf used to be like.

In the midst of this quaintly dilapidated block-long street is a bright red storefront with old-fashioned hand-painted signs on either side of the front door and a Harbor Fish Market sign nailed to the awning above. Stepping into the market is like walking into another world. Straight ahead are two magnificent glass cases fully stocked with all kinds of fresh fish and shellfish. Fish cutters are visible through windows at the back of the store, plying their trade with super-sharp knives.

On the left-hand side of the main floor, next to the shellfish display case, are tables groaning under the weight of fresh whole fish poking out from mounds of ice; a table of wire baskets, each containing various oysters from around New England; and a massive lobster tank holding hundreds of pounds of fresh, live lobsters. Dedicated lobster boats dock daily behind Harbor Fish and offload their catches to the waiting tanks and processing rooms inside.

At any given time there are as many as three full-time employees working the phones and computers in the back offices, sourcing the freshest fish available every day of the year. Harbor Fish truly has its finger on the pulse of the seafood world, and it's constantly working to get the freshest fish and the best deals they can, in order to pass them on to their customers.

With help from his wife and son, Nick has written *Harbor Fish Market,* a delightful collection of the family's seafood recipes and stories developed over the years. It's available for sale at the store, along with a vast array of spices, seafood accompaniments, and seafood-cooking implements.

Visiting Harbor Fish is a walk down memory lane, when fish markets were casual, bustling places in older buildings down by the wharves that people visited every day. This market offers the best in both historical charm and top-shelf seafood, and is well worth a special visit any time of year.

Pan-Fried Soft Shell Crab with Spicy Cilantro Aioli

Wulf's Fish Market, Brookline, Massachusetts

SPICY CILANTRO AIOLI

3 egg yolks

1 ounce Dijon mustard

2 tablespoons lemon juice, strained

2 tablespoons cilantro, chopped

2 tablespoons sriracha

1 tablespoon garlic, finely minced

1 cup olive oil

1 cup vegetable oil (combine the two oils in a pourable container and reserve)

Salt and white pepper to taste

Sea salt and fresh ground pepper to taste

1½ cups all-purpose flour

1 teaspoon cayenne pepper

4 whole soft shell crabs, cleaned

1 cup buttermilk

2 cups vegetable oil

This seasonal treat is made all the more special with Wulf's innovative Spicy Cilantro Aioli as an accompaniment.

To make the aioli, place the egg yolks, mustard, lemon juice, cilantro, sriracha, and garlic in a food processor and let it spin for about 10 seconds. While spinning, gradually pour in the combined oils in a smooth and steady stream until the desired consistency is reached. Adjust the seasoning with salt and white pepper. If the aioli is too thick, you can add more lemon juice or water; if it's too thin, add more oil. Set aside to develop character when it's ready.

To make the softshell crabs, mix the salt, pepper, flour, and cayenne together in a shallow dish. Dredge the crabs in the seasoned flour, submerge each one in buttermilk, then re-dredge them in the flour mixture, shaking off any excess, to get a smooth, even (dry, wet, dry) coating.

Heat the vegetable oil on medium high in a large sauté pan. Once the oil is hot (350 degrees), gently place the crabs in the pan, taking care not to splash the hot oil. Fry the crabs until they are golden brown on each side (approximately 1½ to 2 minutes per side), and remove with a slotted spoon or spatula. Do not overcrowd the pan (cook the crabs in two batches if necessary).

Remove the crabs from the pan and place them gently on a resting rack or clean paper towels to soak up the excess cooking oil. Season with salt and pepper, then serve immediately with lemon, spicy aioli, and a nice tossed salad. Serves 4.

Blackfish with Brown Butter Sauce

Atlantic Seafood, Old Saybrook, Connecticut

1½ tablespoons olive oil

1½ pounds blackfish fillets

¾ cup flour

1–2 tablespoons butter

BROWN BUTTER SAUCE

¼ cup (½ stick) butter

2 tablespoons capers

Juice of ½ lemon

1 tablespoon fresh, chopped
   parsley

Popular with sport fishermen, blackfish is a seasonal delicacy in New England. The fish's plump, meaty fillets are ideal for baking in the oven or for grilling (carefully) on a wood plank outdoors. The brown butter sauce, flavored with capers, goes best with the baked version described here.

Preheat the oven to 375 degrees.

In a skillet over medium high heat, warm the olive oil until it's almost smoking. Dredge the fillets in the flour and place them in the hot skillet. Brown the fillets on both sides, about 2 to 3 minutes each.

Butter a baking dish. Place the browned fillets in the buttered dish, and bake in the preheated oven for about 10 minutes.

To make the brown butter sauce, melt the butter in a small pan over medium heat, cooking it until it starts to brown, about 3 minutes. Add the capers and blend them with the melted, browned butter. Remove the pan from the heat. Add the lemon juice and parsley, then pour the sauce over the blackfish fillets. Serves 4.

Manuela's Octopus

David's Fish Market, Fall River, Massachusetts

1 5-pound whole octopus, cut into bite-size pieces (Portuguese octopus preferred)

1 large onion, diced

3 garlic cloves, minced

1 8-ounce can tomato sauce

½ teaspoon white pepper

1 tablespoon garlic powder

3 tablespoons olive oil

¼ cup red wine

4 large potatoes, cubed

This Portuguese dish is quite simple to make and brings together the various flavors and textures of fresh octopus, tomato, garlic, and wine, for a heady roasted seafood stew.

Preheat the oven to 400 degrees. Add all the ingredients except the potatoes to a roasting pan, and mix together. Bake for 30 minutes, then remove it from the oven and add the potatoes. Bake the dish for another 30 minutes, or until the potatoes are cooked through. Serves 6 to 8.

David's Fish Market

Fall River, Massachusetts

The Sardinha family has been running this quaint little fish market—which lies smack-dab in the middle of Fall River's Portuguese community—for decades, and it's now well into its second generation of family ownership. Housed in a modest storefront in a mostly residential part of the city, David's has been providing fresh, Portuguese-style seafood to the locals for over fifty years.

Lazaro and Maria Sardinha started David's as a retail market in 1961, and in the 1970s they expanded into the wholesale business, visiting the docks of Fall River each day and buying fish and shellfish right off the boat. They also happen to be just up the road from New Bedford, one of the largest commercial fishing ports in the nation, so there's never been a lack of good product with which to stock their store.

In the market's seafood cases you'll find such staples as cod, scrod, haddock, sole, mackerel, salmon, swordfish, hake, redfish, sea bass, tilapia, and scup. Seasonal specialties, such as striped bass and bluefish, are also often available. Then there are the Portuguese specialties, flown in from the Azores on a regular basis, such as chicharros (a type of mackerel) and garoupa (grouper).

Virtually all types of New England clams (littlenecks, steamers, cherrystones, quahogs, and more) are available at David's year-round. Large, live lobsters swim in a tank by one of the store's front windows. Live crabs are often available, as well as fresh-picked lobster meat and crabmeat for soups, sauces, chowders, and rolls. Sea scallops (year-round) and bay scallops (in the winter months) are other popular choices.

David's is heavily frequented by the surrounding Portuguese-American population, who reside in the many white-washed, multifamily dwellings that sit hard by immaculately clean streets. The Portuguese community has roots in the commercial fishing industry that stretch back more than a hundred years in southeastern Massachusetts and eastern Rhode Island. It's a proud community—one that values its traditions and heritage, and its love of the sea lives on in this gem of a seafood market.

Manuela Sardinha

Bacalhau à Brás

David's Fish Market, Fall River, Massachusetts

2 pounds salted boneless codfish

2 cups vegetable oil

6 large potatoes, cut into thin, matchstick-size pieces (a potato ricer works well)

¾ cup olive oil

4 large onions, chopped

1 cup parsley leaves, chopped

8 eggs, beaten

What do you get when you combine salted cod, fried potatoes, and scrambled eggs? Bacalhau à Brás, of course! This unusual and alluring Portuguese dish from Manuela Sardinha at David's Fish Market, in Fall River, Massachusetts, is a favorite comfort food in Portuguese households.

Before cooking, soak the salted cod overnight in several changes of cool water.

On the stovetop, boil the codfish in a pot of heated water until softened. Remove the codfish from the water and let it cool, then shred to fine bits by hand. Set it aside.

Place the vegetable oil in a heavy pot or skillet, and heat until approximately 350 degrees. Cook the potato shreds until they're lightly golden, about 2 minutes. Remove the potatoes from the pan with a slotted spoon, and place them on double layers of paper towels to cool and drain (cooking the potatoes will need to be done in several batches).

In a separate, large frying pan or pot, heat the olive oil over medium heat. Cook the onions in the oil until they're translucent. Add the codfish, stir well, then add the fried potatoes and continue stirring.

Mix the parsley in with the beaten eggs, and pour the mixture into the pot or pan with the other ingredients. Cook, stirring, until the eggs reach a scrambled consistency. Once the eggs are cooked, add a bit more olive oil for flavor, if desired, stir one last time, and serve hot. Serves 8 to 10.

MARINADES, SAUCES, AND STUFFINGS

Nauset Fish and Lobster Pool

Orleans, Massachusetts

Right in the crook of the arm formed by the Cape Cod landmass lies the town of Orleans. In a tiny strip mall on Route 6A, you'll find Sir Cricket's Fish and Chips, one of the more renowned seafood takeout joints on the Cape, and next door to Cricket's is the equally renowned Nauset Fish and Lobster Pool fish market.

Owned and operated by the Harrison family, Nauset Fish and Lobster Pool is one of the Cape's most popular and well-known seafood markets. In 1965, Herbert Harrison started out at Young's Fish Market in nearby Rock Harbor before expanding into Nauset Fish and Lobster Pool and Sir Cricket's Fish and Chips. Today, his granddaughter Rebecca holds the same high standards that have made Nauset Fish and Lobster Pool and Sir Cricket's Cape Cod favorites: fresh fish, lobster, and shellfish, all at great prices.

The fresh fish displays at Nauset Fish are a veritable smorgasbord of seafood offer-

ings, with trays of fish and shellfish stacked three- and four-deep behind the glass partitions. Feast your eyes on the likes of fresh cod, haddock, bluefish, halibut, swordfish steaks, sea scallops, sole, tuna, squid, and arctic char. There's also smoked salmon and bluefish in fillet and pâté forms, as well as smoked mussels.

This is also the mid-Cape's go-to place for fresh, meaty, live lobsters, which are brought in from local boats daily. Don't want to cook your own? There's plenty of fresh-picked lobster meat in the case, next to a few different varieties of fresh-

cooked or raw jumbo shrimp. Fresh clams and mussels also abound, great for steaming at home or adding to your favorite pasta sauce. Lobster-stuffed sole is one of the more popular prepared foods available at Nauset Fish.

The back and side walls of the concrete-floored market are lined with a small but fine selection of wines and a couple refrigerated cases stocked with beer. You won't go wanting for much after shopping here, and you can always grab a plate of award-winning fish and chips at Sir Cricket's next door, before or after you've made your seafood purchases.

Citrus-Mint Bluefish Marinade

Nauset Fish and Lobster Pool, Orleans, Massachusetts

2 limes, freshly squeezed

1 tablespoon olive oil

2 tablespoons soy sauce

2 medium garlic cloves, minced

¼ cup dry white wine

2 tablespoons fresh mint leaves

1 pound bluefish fillets

For many, bluefish is an acquired taste, with its pungent natural flavor and its oily texture. This marinade brings out the best the fish has to offer, and for many it masks some of the fish's less desirable qualities. It's a great way to introduce yourself to this most challenging of native New England species.

To make the marinade, combine all the ingredients except the fish in a bowl. Score the fish skin and place the fillets in a shallow baking dish. Pour the marinade over the fillets, and flip the fillets several times to coat both sides. Put the marinating fillets in the refrigerator for 1½ to 2 hours. During that time, flip the fillets several more times, spooning marinade over the tops.

After the fillets are done marinating, grill them over medium-high heat for 8 to 10 minutes, flipping once. Serves 2.

Atlantic Seafood Dill Topper

Atlantic Seafood, Old Saybrook, Connecticut

3 cups mayonnaise

1 cup sour cream

4 tablespoons Vidalia onion, diced

2 tablespoons dill, finely chopped

Juice of 1 lemon

1 tablespoon hot sauce

Atlantic Seafood chef Jerry Doran recommends this all-purpose topper for fish of virtually any type. Whip some together and use on your fresh-cooked or leftover seafood. It's also great on fresh vegetables and as a dip for chips.

Mix all the ingredients together well, then set aside and chill for an hour or so to let the flavors come together. Makes 8 to 10 seafood toppings or 1 bowl of dip.

Jerry Doran of Atlantic Seafood

New Deal Fish Market

Cambridge, Massachusetts

This storefront seafood shop in East Cambridge, Massachusetts, has been in business since 1928, and is frequently voted the number one place to get fresh fish in the Boston area. Why? One look at the seafood case usually answers that question. New Deal Fish Market has one of the most splendid and unique offerings of finned fish to be found anywhere in New England. Making regular appearances are such specialties as scup, European sea bass, spotted red snapper, sea bream, locally caught striped bass and bluefish, and much more. Even better, most of these fish are available whole.

Carl Fantasia is the enthusiastic and energetic owner of the market, which has been in his family from the beginning. Carl is a walking, talking encyclopedia of fish knowledge, and his staff is equally well versed in all things seafood. One of the reasons for the market's eclectic offerings is the multiethnic makeup of the East Cambridge neighborhood. All sorts of people come in with particular needs, and Carl and his staff do their best to fulfill them. They are on a first-name basis with most of the regular customers, and they often remember what each customer purchased on their last visit. It's this kind of service that keeps people coming here rather than seeking out their seafood needs at Whole Foods or elsewhere.

The market has a genuine and old-fashioned feel to it, with mounds of fresh produce in front of the seafood case and well-stocked wooden shelves that line the shop's walls. There are bottles of exotic olive oils, interesting and unusual spices and seasonings, and canned and jarred seafood specialties, such as sardines, ventresca tuna in olive oil, and marinated anchovies. Italian specialties, such as polenta and northern beans, are stocked in the market's dry-goods section.

Sushi and sashimi are big deals at New Deal, and a large portion of the market's business involves selling the raw ingredients for these Japanese specialties. As a boon to customers, most of the fish labels in the seafood case carry the Japanese-equivalent words for each fish species. In addition, there is a broad array of sushi-making products in one section of the store—such as various types of soy sauces and rice vinegars, sushi rice, dried seaweed wraps, rice noodles, and Japanese canola oil.

Seasonal shellfish specialties include such fun things as crawfish, oysters, and soft-shell crabs, while shrimp, scallops, lobsters, and clams are available pretty much year-round. A small selection of imported gourmet cheeses rounds out the store's offerings.

New Deal Fish Market encompasses pretty much everything a good seafood market should. If you're fortunate enough to live nearby, by all means frequent the place on a regular basis. If you don't, it's still worth a special trip. Carl and his staff will gladly put your order on ice for transport near or far, and if you're lucky, they'll remember your name and what you ordered the next time you come.

Soy and Maple Marinade

New Deal Fish Market, Cambridge, Massachusetts

4 tablespoons soy sauce

3 tablespoons real maple syrup (use 2 tablespoons for less sweetness)

1 tablespoon Dijon mustard

1 tablespoon olive oil

1–2 garlic cloves, chopped

¼ teaspoon thyme

This recipe is used for a one-pound fillet of a rich, fatty fish. The fish that New Deal Fish Market's Carl Fantasia typically uses with this marinade are salmon, Alaskan black cod, Chilean sea bass, or swordfish.

Combine all the ingredients in a bowl, and whisk until the ingredients are mixed together well.

Place a fish fillet in a shallow, square food storage container and pour the contents of the marinade on top of the fish. Make sure the fish is well coated with the marinade, and then cover the container. Place the container in the refrigerator and let the fish marinate for approximately 45 minutes.

Place the marinated fillets on a broiling pan and broil in the oven until the top of the fillet is well caramelized and cooked to a dark brown color, approximately 5 to 7 minutes. Once the top is cooked, the middle portion of the fillet may still be raw or very rare.

If you wish to cook the fish through, turn off the oven and let the fillet remain inside the warm oven for an additional 3–5 minutes. Serve immediately after cooking. This recipe makes enough marinade for a 1 to 1½-pound fillet.
Serves 2 to 3.

Wasabi Topper

Atlantic Seafood, Old Saybrook, Connecticut

1½ teaspoons wasabi powder

4 tablespoons water

2 tablespoons mirin (a Japanese rice wine)

3 tablespoons soy sauce (light)

1 tablespoon mustard powder

1 tablespoon rice wine vinegar

1 tablespoon olive oil

¼ teaspoon honey

Juice of 4 limes

Here's a nice topper with a Japanese flair. It goes particularly well with raw or seared tuna, sushi, or grilled fish.

Mix all the ingredients together well. Set aside for at least an hour to let the flavors come together.

Grandma David's Oyster Stuffing

David's Fish Market and Lobster Pound, Salisbury, Massachusetts

2 tablespoons olive oil

1 medium sweet onion, chopped

2–3 celery stalks, chopped

1 pound sausage, out of casing
  (any type of sausage from the
  meat section or butcher works)

1 quart oysters, shucked, with
  liquid

2 loaves white bread

Salt

Pepper

Poultry seasoning

This is a family favorite at Thanksgiving for David's Fish Market owner Gordon Blaney, his wife, Lynette, and their next of kin.

Preheat the oven to 375 degrees. In a large skillet, heat the olive oil over medium heat, then sauté the onion until it's transparent. Add the celery and sausage and continue cooking until the sausage is browned. Add the oysters, along with the liquid they came in. Remove the skillet from the heat, spoon the contents into a bowl, and set it aside.

In a large bowl, tear the bread into small, bite-size pieces. Fold in the onion, sausage, and oyster mixture, and mix everything together until it forms a sticky mass (add more bread if the mixture is too moist). Add salt, pepper, and poultry seasoning to taste, and mix thoroughly.

Spoon the mixture into a casserole dish lightly coated with vegetable oil or Pam spray, and bake for 45 minutes.

Tip: For a firmer stuffing, cube the white bread a few days in advance, and let it sit out in the open air to stiffen up a bit before using in the stuffing.

Hog Wash (Mac's Famous Oyster Mignonette Sauce)

Mac's Seafood, Wellfleet, Massachusetts

1 cup jalapeño pepper, finely diced

1 cup red Fresno chili, finely diced (Serrano pepper is a decent substitute)

½ cup cilantro, chopped

½ cup shallot, finely diced

1 lime

1½ cups seasoned rice wine vinegar

1½ cups unseasoned rice wine vinegar

½ tablespoon fresh ground pepper

Wellfleet, Massachusetts, home of Mac's Seafood, is world famous for its oysters. This quaint Outer Cape town, just south of Provincetown, is annual home to the raucous Wellfleet Oyster Festival. Whether you make it to the festival or not, Mac's Hog Wash makes for a great complement to oysters of any origin or type. Try it out on a bunch of oysters from your local seafood market, and see what you think.

Remove the seeds and core from the jalapeño pepper and red Fresno chili, and dice them small. Clean the cilantro and lightly chop it. Dice the shallots, and zest and juice the lime. Mix all the ingredients together in a bowl with the seasoned and unseasoned rice wine vinegars, and peppers, and let the sauce rest for 30 minutes to allow the flavors to bloom.

When the sauce is done resting, grab a spoon and splash it over freshly shucked oysters. There should be enough to cover a few dozen oysters. Store any leftover sauce in a sealed container in the refrigerator. Hog Wash only gets better with age.

Tip: Seasoned rice wine vinegar is made by adding sugar and salt (or sometimes sake) to plain white rice vinegar. Commercially produced bottles of seasoned rice wine vinegar are clearly labeled as "seasoned" and are available in most markets where regular rice wine vinegar is sold.

Mike's Fish Market and Lobster Pound

Wells, Maine

The large, well-known family restaurant called Mike's Clam Shack sits on a busy stretch of Route 1 in Wells, Maine, not too far from the ocean. It has grown over the years into a sprawling series of small buildings, serving excellent fried clams, locally caught lobsters, and other seafood.

In 2006, owner Mike McDermott decided to add a seafood market and lobster pound to his restaurant operation, and it started in a small building next to the restaurant that used to be the office of a motel. Things went well for the fish market under the watchful eye of manager Barney Rich, and eventually the market relocated to a larger building about fifty yards away, making it clearly a stand-alone business separate from the restaurant.

Mike's Fish Market and Lobster Pound is a busy place, especially in the summertime, offering fresh cod, haddock, halibut, swordfish, tuna, sea scallops, and raw and cooked shrimp. They're particularly proud of the organic, farm-raised salmon that they bring in almost daily from Scotland. Fresh-baked breads and pies from local bakers are daily features at the market.

The other two standout items are the live lobsters and the clam chowder. The multi-tiered lobster tanks line the back wall of the market, and Mike's will cook up your lobsters for take-away. The chowder, which is based on the recipe from Mike's Clam Shack, is rich and creamy and cooked up daily. You may also purchase Mike's Clam Chowder Kit, three cans of chowder and chopped clams to which you simply add milk or cream, heat, and serve.

This is a spot to keep in mind if you're vacationing in Wells or nearby Ogunquit. There's not a better place for fresh seafood in this popular stretch of southern Maine.

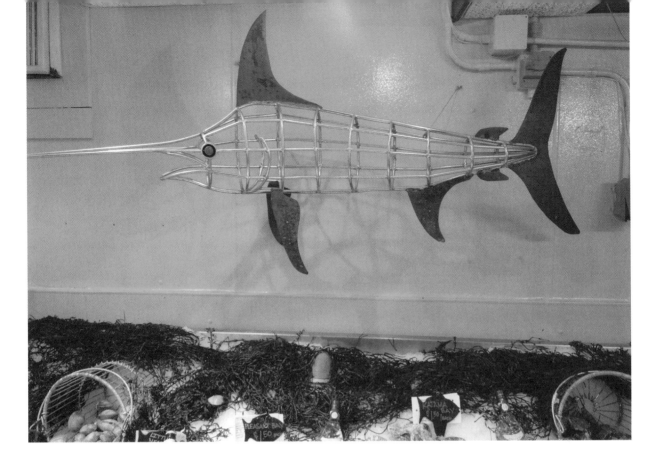

Swordfish Marinade

Nauset Fish and Lobster Pool, Orleans, Massachusetts

Juice of 3 lemons

¼ cup olive oil

2 tablespoons Dijon mustard

¼ cup fresh dill

¼ teaspoon salt

Black pepper to taste

1 clove garlic, minced

1 pound swordfish fillets

The Dijon mustard and dill give this marinade its distinctive, zesty flavor. It's a great complement to fresh swordfish, especially when cooked on the grill.

Mix the ingredients together and place the fillets in the marinade. Place the marinating fillets in the refrigerator for 1 to 2 hours. When they're finished marinating, grill the fillets over high heat for 5 to 7 minutes per side. Serves 2.

Tip: You may substitute halibut, striped bass, or salmon for the fillets, but swordfish is one of the easier and more forgiving fish fillets for grilling.

Mary's Fish Marinade

David's Fish Market and Lobster Pound, Salisbury, Massachusetts

1½ cups cooking oil

½ cup soy sauce

⅓ cup red wine vinegar

⅓ cup brown sugar

1 heaping tablespoon garlic, minced, or garlic powder

1 medium sweet onion, minced

This homemade marinade works particularly well with larger, meatier fish fillets, such as halibut or swordfish.

Mix all the ingredients together in a bowl, and then pour them into a large Ziplock bag. Put 1 to 2 pounds of fish fillets in the bag, seal, and let them marinate in the refrigerator for at least 1 hour. When finished, discard the marinade and grill or bake the fish.

Chouriço Stuffing

Anthony's Seafood, Middletown, Rhode Island

1 large onion, diced

2 garlic cloves, minced

1 pound ground chouriço sausage

Splashes of white wine, to moisten

2 eggs, beaten

1½ cups breadcrumbs

This traditional Portuguese item is made with chouriço (pronounced shore-EEZ) sausage. It's a spicy, flavorful stuffing for baked fish fillets like haddock, cod, and hake.

In a skillet over medium heat, cook the onions, garlic, and chouriço until the sausage is fully browned. Add a splash of wine, remove from the heat, and spoon the mixture into a large bowl. Add the eggs and breadcrumbs and mix together, adding more breadcrumbs and wine until the desired consistency is achieved. Makes 5 to 6 servings.

Essex Seafood

Essex, Massachusetts

On Route 133 in Essex, Massachusetts (also known as the "Clam Highway" because of the great clam shacks along the route), Essex Seafood occupies a modest space in the back of a white-washed colonial house that probably dates back a couple hundred years.

The primary draw here is the dine-in-the-rough eatery, featuring cooked lobsters and deep-fried seafood; but there's also a small seafood market attached to the restaurant, where one may procure whole lobsters to take home and small catches of the day (haddock, scallops, and the like) from local day boats. There's a big red-and-white sign by the road, so if you feel tempted or are in need of something for dinner, pull in and check it out. It's open year-round.

Black and Blue Vinaigrette

McLaughlin's Seafood, Bangor, Maine

1 lemon

1 cup blueberries

¼ cup blackberries

½ cup virgin olive oil

1 cup vegetable oil

¾ cup balsamic vinegar

¼ cup brown sugar

1 tablespoon thyme, diced

1½ tablespoons soy sauce

Salt and pepper to taste

This salad dressing is a favorite at McLaughlin's at the Marina, the supper club extension of McLaughlin's Seafood. The restaurant is in nearby Hampden and sits along the banks of the Penobscot River, allowing boaters to tie up and duck inside for lunch or dinner. The berries in this recipe add a tart, fruity flavor to the dressing. When possible, use fresh Maine berries when they're in season.

Roll the lemon, then zest and juice it. Combine all the ingredients into a large cruet or other suitable container with a lid and pour spout. Close the lid, and gently shake until the contents are thoroughly blended. Yields enough dressing for several large group salads.

New England Seafood Markets Directory

Al's Seafood
51 Lafayette Rd.
North Hampton, NH 03862
(603) 964-9591
www.alsseafoodnh.com

Anthony's Seafood
963 Aquidneck Ave.
Middletown, RI 02842
(401) 846-9620
www.anthonysseafood.net

Atlantic Seafood
1400 Boston Post Rd.
Old Saybrook, CT 06475
(860) 388-4527
www.atlanticseafoodmarket.com

Bayley's Lobster Pound
9 Avenue 6
Scarborough, ME 04074
(207) 883-4571
www.bayleys.com

Blount Market
406 Water St.
Warren, RI 02885
(401) 245-1800
www.blountretail.com

Boothbay Lobster Wharf
97 Atlantic Ave.
Boothbay Harbor, ME 04538
(207) 633-4900
www.boothbaylobsterwharf.com

Browne Trading Company
262 Commercial St.
Portland, ME 04101
(207) 775-7560
www.brownetrading.com

Bud's Fish Market
4 Sybil Ave.
Branford, CT 06405
(203) 348-1019
www.budsfishmarket.com

Cape Codder Seafood Market
679 Route 28
West Yarmouth, MA 02673
(508) 775-0054
www.capecodderseafoodmarket.com

Captain Scott's Lobster Dock
80 Hamilton St.
New London, CT 06320
(860) 439-1741
www.captscotts.com

Champlin's Seafood
256 Great Island Rd.
Narragansett, RI 02882
(401) 783-3152
www.champlins.com

Chatham Pier Fish Market
45 Briarcliff Ave. Ext.
Chatham, MA 02633
(508) 945-3474
www.chathampierfishmarket.com

City Fish Market
884 Silas Deane Hwy.
Wethersfield, CT 06109
(860) 522-3129
www.cfishct.com

Clam Shack Seafood Market
5 Western Ave.
Kennebunk, ME 04046
(207) 967-3321
www.theclamshack.net

David's Fish Market
257 Davis St.
Fall River, MA 02720
(508) 676-1221
www.davidsfish.com

David's Fish Market and Lobster Pound
54 Bridge Rd.
Salisbury, MA 01952
(978) 462-2504
www.davidsfishmarket.com

Donahue's Fish Market
20 Plaistow Rd.
Plaistow, NH 03865
(603) 382-6181
www.donahuesfishmarket.com

Essex Seafood
143 Eastern Ave.
Essex, MA 01929
(978) 768-7233
www.essexseafood.com

Fisherman's Catch
49 Main St.
Damariscotta, ME 04543
(207) 563-5888
[no website]

Flanders Fish Market
22 Chesterfield Rd.
East Lyme, CT 06333
(860) 739-8866
www.flandersfish.com

Free Range Fish and Lobster
450 Commercial St.
Portland, ME 04101
(207) 774-8469
www.freerangefish.com

Friendly Fisherman
4580 Route 6
North Eastham, MA 02651
(508) 255-3009
www.friendlyfishermaneastham.com

Gardner's Wharf Seafood
170 Main St.
Wickford, RI 02852
(401) 295-4600
www.gardnerswharfseafood.com

Harbor Fish Market
9 Custom House Wharf
Portland, ME 04101
(207) 775-0251
www.harborfish.com

Hatch's Fish Market
310 Main St.
Wellfleet, MA 02667
(508) 349-2810
www.hatchsfishmarket.com

Jess's Market
118 S. Main St.
Rockland, ME 04841
(207) 596-6068
www.jessmarket.com

Kyler's Seafood
2 Washburn St.
New Bedford, MA 02740
(508) 984-5150
www.kylerseafood.com

Mac's Seafood Market
265 Commercial St.
Wellfleet, MA 02667
(508) 349-0404
(3 other locations)
www.macsseafood.com

McLaughlin Seafood
728 Main St.
Bangor, ME 04401
(207) 942-7811
www.mclaughlinseafood.com

Mike's Clam Shack Seafood Market
1150 Post Rd.
Wells, ME 04090
(207) 646-5998
www.mikesclamshack.com

Nauset Fish and Lobster Pool
38 Route 6A
Orleans, MA 02653
(508) 255-1019
www.nausetfish.com

New Deal Fish Market
622 Cambridge St.
Cambridge, MA 02141
(617) 876-8227
www.newdealfishmarket.com

Pinkham's Seafood
798 Wiscasset Rd.
Boothbay, ME 04537
(207) 633-6236
www.pinkhamsseafood.com

**Port Clyde Fresh Catch
Fish Cooperative**
18 Lobster Pound Rd.
Port Clyde, ME 04855
(207) 372-1055
www.portclydefreshcatch.com

Port Lobster Company
122 Ocean Ave.
Kennebunkport, ME 04046
(207) 967-2081
www.portlobster.com

R&D Seafood
652 Smithfield Rd.
Woonsocket, RI 02895
(401) 769-1078
www.rdseafood.com

Sanders Fish Market
367 Marcy St.
Portsmouth, NH 03801
(603) 436-4568
www.sandersfish.com

Seaport Fish
13 Sagamore Rd.
Rye, NH 03870
(603) 436-7286
www.seaportfish.com

Star Fish Market
650 Village Walk
Guilford, CT 06437
(203) 458-3474
www.starfishmkt.com

Superior Seafood
999 Post Rd. East
Westport, CT 06880
(203) 557-0844
www.westportsuperiorseafood.com

Trenton Bridge Lobster Pound
1237 Bar Harbor Rd.
Trenton, ME 04605
(207) 667-2977
www.trentonbridgelobster.com

Turner's Seafood
4 Smith St.
Gloucester, MA 01930
(978) 281-8535
www.turners-seafood.com

Wulf's Fish Market
409 Harvard St.
Brookline, MA 02446
(617& 277-2506
[no website]

Index